CUPID CARDS

The Oracle of Love

CELEBRATE
Celebrate life every day.

UNDERSTAND
Understand yourself and make an effort to understand others.

PEACE
Peace begins when expectations end.

INTUITION
Intuition is your inner vision. Let it guide you to your goal.

DECISION
Poor decision making is the cause of much emotional suffering.

CHERISH
Cherish yourself and your partner. You are each other's wealth.

ART
Art tells you as much about yourself as about the work of art.

REALITY
Reality is created by our belief system.

DON'T WORRY
Worry only creates stress and accomplishes nothing.

SAVOR
Savor the present moment. It is all the time you really have.

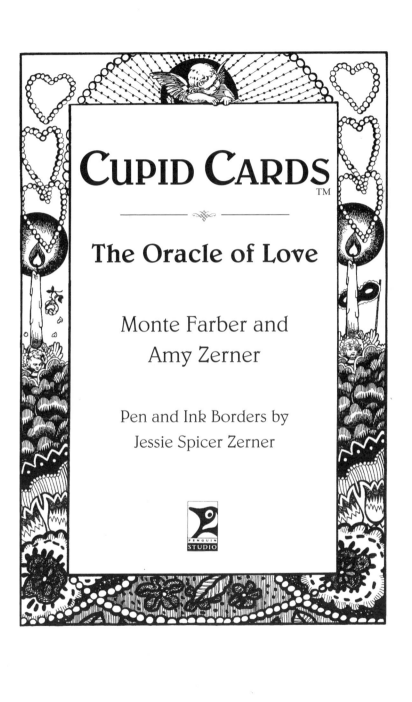

CUPID CARDS™

The Oracle of Love

Monte Farber and
Amy Zerner

Pen and Ink Borders by
Jessie Spicer Zerner

PENGUIN
STUDIO

PENGUIN STUDIO
Published by the Penguin Group
Penguin Books USA Inc., 375 Hudson Street,
New York, New York 10014, U.S.A.
Penguin Books Ltd, 27 Wrights Lane, London W8 5TZ, England
Penguin Books Australia Ltd, Ringwood, Victoria, Australia
Penguin Books Canada Ltd, 10 Alcorn Avenue,
Toronto, Ontario, Canada M4V 3B2
Penguin Books (N.Z.) Ltd, 182–190 Wairau Road,
Auckland 10, New Zealand

Penguin Books Ltd, Registered Offices:
Harmondsworth, Middlesex, England

First published in 1996 by Viking Penguin,
a division of Penguin Books USA Inc.

1 3 5 7 9 10 8 6 4 2

Cupid Cards™ is a trademark of Monte Farber and Amy Zerner.

ISBN 0–670–85747–5

Printed in Hong Kong

Set in Belwe Light
Designed by Kathryn Parise

CONTENTS

———— ❧ ————

INTRODUCTION

*Make love your great quest; then desire spiritual gifts, and
especially that you may prophecy.*

—I CORINTHIANS 14:1

For more than two thousand years the name Cupid has been
synonymous with romantic love. Cupid was the name given to
the ancient god, Eros, by the Romans when they adopted the
Greek pantheon and made them the gods of the Roman Empire.
In Roman mythology, Cupid was the son of Venus, goddess
of love, and Mercury, the god of communication. With such
parents, Cupid was perfectly suited to be the young god who
communicated love to the world.

Since the Renaissance of the fifteenth century, artists have
used the image of that most adorable cherubic angel with his
love-dispensing bow and arrow as the symbol for the divine force
that can manifest romantic love. It is important to note that Cupid has not always been depicted as a very young child or even
exclusively as male.

In the CUPID CARDS deck, Amy Zerner, my wife of twenty years
and a leading collage artist, has depicted Cupid in his myriad
forms. You will most often see her unique portraits of the young
god of love as the mischievous infant that we are all so familiar
with, but you will also encounter his male and female manifestations at different stages of life.

Like Cupid, CUPID CARDS is the product of the union of Venus
and Mercury as Amy and I have joined her art to my words.
Also similar is that this coupling has produced a "child" whose
life's purpose is to help you find love and the answers to
love's questions.

For thousands of years, those seeking wisdom from divine forces have consulted oracles. A famous one was the oracle of the sun god, Apollo on the Greek island of Delphi. It was there that the expression "Know thyself" was found inscribed on one of the two great pillars flanking the temple's entrance. On the other was the equally wise but lesser known admonition, "Nothing in excess."

Like the human oracles, who had to spend most of their lifetimes absorbing the knowledge of the ancient Mystery Schools before they could dispense the word of the gods and goddesses, Amy and I have spent much of our lives studying and practicing the knowledge and wisdom of the ancient schools. We have applied what we have learned as designers of interactive personal guidance systems. CUPID CARDS is the culmination of our studies. It is our most sincere desire that working with CUPID CARDS empowers you and helps you find the way to happiness and true love.

The closest thing to an explanation of how and why CUPID CARDS, or any oracles, work is an ancient principle rediscovered in the twentieth century by pioneering psychologist Carl Jung. Jung called it synchronicity (from the Greek syn, meaning "together," and chronos meaning "time"). He postulated that things that happen at the same time have a relationship of significance even though they do not cause each other to happen. This meaningful coincidence of outer events, such as the appearance of a particular card in a reading, and inner thoughts, feelings, or ideas explains the accuracy of oracles and astrology. Like a hologram, each piece of the universe contains all the information necessary to create the whole universe. Throughout the universe everything is connected to everything else. This interconnection and interdependence of all things is a basic premise of many philosophies, mythologies, and religions.

Cupid Cards is your personal, beautifully illustrated, and portable shrine dedicated to Cupid. It is also the medium through which you can receive answers to your questions about bringing true love into your life and keeping it. Like any oracle, Cupid Cards causes us to use a combination of our intuition and logical mind. Intuition enables us to receive and decode information while our mind puts the information in a context that can be understood and communicated through language. This combination once again symbolizes the union of Venus and Mercury.

Much of what causes emotional pain and suffering can be avoided by clearer thinking and better decision making. Like the value of true love, the value of proper decision making is one of the few things which everyone can agree upon. The mystic would say that we create our own reality and, therefore, what we decide to create will determine what we experience. The more traditionally religious person would say that deciding whether or not to be aware of our eternal oneness with the Divine will determine whether or not we will suffer life's trials and tribulations with healing and acceptance or with pain and rage. The practical business person would say that our decision-making ability determines how much power we will accumulate on our brief journey through life on Earth—the more power we possess, the happier we will be.

Being constantly assaulted with the thousand and one challenges of daily life makes it difficult for us to hear our inner voice, which some people call the voice of our higher self. The gentle ritual of consulting the Cupid Cards allows us to create the time and space in our life that, in turn, allows us to remember what we all know deep within us.

CUPID CARDS provides you with the means for getting in touch with the quiet voice within you that knows, without a doubt, what is best for your greatest good and highest joy. Geared specifically to matters of the heart, CUPID CARDS is a tool to help you make the decisions that you need to improve your existing relationship or to meet someone new. It works on a heart-and-soul level to provide clear and insightful answers to your questions. Whether it is used as a lighthearted party game or in moments of quiet reflection, CUPID CARDS can reveal unconscious beliefs about love, both those that draw love to us as well as those that keep us from the real love that is our birthright.

There is an art to bringing love into one's life. There are specific steps one can take to do so. We have created CUPID CARDS to acquaint you with the art of love and to show you the steps to meet your soul mate. CUPID CARDS can light your way there.

—Monte Farber
East Hampton, N.Y., 1996

Instructions for Use

I. How to Arrange the Cupid Cards Deck

To use the thirty-six CUPID CARDS place the three color-coded stacks of twelve cards each before you with the images facing up. Each deck is identified by the border of color on each side of the card. The three stacks of twelve cards each are known as the Amethyst, Ruby, and Turquoise decks and MUST be arranged, with the image side facing up, in this order:

AMETHYST	RUBY	TURQUOISE
on the LEFT	in the MIDDLE	on the RIGHT

It is easy to remember in what order the three stacks go. All you have to do is remember that, just as Cupid is the product of the union of Venus and Mercury, CUPID CARDS represents the marriage of ART and words (ART =Amethyst, Ruby, Turquoise).

II. How to Phrase Your Question

There are two basic questions for CUPID CARDS. They are:

How can I bring love into my life? and How can I make my relationship better? There are also several variations:

How can I find my soul mate?
How should I be with my love interest in order to accomplish my goal?
How should I respond to the idea of a relationship with this person at this time?
What do I need to work on to improve my chance of having a love relationship?
What are the main issues that are keeping me from meeting my soul mate?
Can (or should) my relationship be saved?

Keep in mind that no one knows your situation better than you do. You may come up with a way to phrase your question that is more appropriate. Using Cupid Cards is about learning to trust yourself and your ability to make decisions for yourself. You are encouraged to be as creative with the use of Cupid Cards as you can be, even if this means that you invent new ways to use the cards.

III. Receiving the Information

Pick up the Amethyst stack, close your eyes and take a deep, luxurious breath. Visualize the situation you are asking about. As you take a second, relaxing breath, see you and the person in question facing each other. Finally, as you take your third deep breath, see Cupid hovering above the two of you, smiling his impish smile. Believe with all your heart that Cupid knows exactly what you must do to achieve the loving relationship he knows you deserve. Through Cupid Cards he will tell you.

Next, as you shuffle the first stack (Amethyst), with eyes closed, ask Cupid your question, either silently to yourself or aloud. Put the first stack down with the image facing right side up, and repeat your question as you shuffle the second (Ruby) and finally the third stack (Turquoise) in the same manner.

When you have finished shuffling the three stacks individually you will see before you a beautiful triptych formed by the three images on the back of the top card of each of the three stacks of Cupid Cards. Feast your eyes on the artwork that makes up the symbolic portion of the answer to your question. Symbolic images are the language of our dream state and our subconscious mind. Allow the images you have summoned to penetrate your psyche and prepare you to receive the verbal guidance that will follow.

Turning over the top card of each stack reveals text divided into two sections. The top section of each card summarizes the poem below it and gives advice about what you should do to accomplish your goal. This advice is recommended specifically for your question. The bottom section contains the poem that identifies those key issues and subtle forces at work which must be identified to attain the relationship of your dreams.

If you would like to gain further insight into your situation and into the advice that Cupid Cards is offering you, you may look up the deeper meaning of each card in this book. First read the description and significance of the scene depicted on the image side of each card. You will find that the symbolic meaning of these images will trigger insights into your situation from your higher self which, like your dream state, communicates with you in the language of symbols. Following that will be another section about each card called "The Heart of the Matter," which offers insight on what may have caused this area of life to be a problem. You will also find specific advice which, when put into action, can help you accomplish your goal.

IV. Sample Questions and Answers

QUESTION 1

A woman in her mid-thirties has had several relationships over the years, and the two most serious ones did not work out. The first man was not ready for a commitment when she was, and the second man had a secret drinking problem. She cut off each relationship. She has been lonely recently and worries that she will never meet "Mr. Right." Still, she has been patiently working on herself, seeing a therapist, and developing her career as a music teacher, and she has many wonderful friends.

She asks CUPID CARDS, "What are the main issues that keep me from meeting my soul mate?" The answer:

The Jeweller...   Endures...   The Past...

CUPID CARDS is telling her not to worry, that soon her wish for a fulfilling relationship will be granted if she keeps doing as she has been doing. The appearance of the Jeweler also means that her greatest challenge at this time is to maintain a positive attitude even though things do not seem to be going the way she would like. The challenge to maintain a positive attitude is reinforced by Endures. She must be able to wait whatever short time it will take for love to enter her life. This card, in conjunction with the final card, the Past, can also be a warning not to let the habits picked up from having to endure disappointment in her relationships in the past affect what is on the horizon. On the whole, the reading tells her the welcome news that love is near so she must only be be patient.

QUESTION 2

A forty-five-year-old man has just gotten out of a four-year relationship. He has gone on numerous dates but has been unable to find anyone with whom he would like to make a lasting commitment, even though he says he would like to.

He asks CUPID CARDS, "How can I bring true love into my life?" The answer:

The Storyteller...   Loves...   The Future...

Although the man is very gregarious and outgoing, and shares his feelings easily, the Storyteller reminds him to pay attention to others when they try to tell him their story. He admitted that a recent incident in his life—an argument with a new love interest—showed him that he has to pay more attention to his listening skills. The Loves card helped him to realize that he has waited so long for the right partner only because he is not willing to settle for less. This relieved a lot of his guilt about his perceived "failure" to find his soul mate.

He feels open to the Future—perhaps a bit too open—specially since the message from the Loves card indicated that something good was about to happen. When he looked at the short sentence formed by the key words of the three cards, "The Storyteller . . . Loves . . . The Future," he gained another insight into a personality trait that may have been blocking him in his quest for love. He interpreted this simple sentence as an indication that he has a tendency to always look toward the future to produce someone better than who he is with in the present. He suddenly realized that this attitude was preventing him from really being with anyone. This is a good example of how even simple sentences can awaken important realizations within us.

V. A Gentle Reminder

Remember that the answer to your question is your own answer and no one else's. When and if you ever choose to use CUPID CARDS in the presence of others, you will be amazed at how often the same answer means something different to everyone else. Sometimes, everybody <u>but</u> the person who asked the question will understand the answer. It will be obvious that the person asking the question is refusing to see what is plain to everyone else. Be gentle with him or her; people are vulnerable when it comes to matters of love. Everyone participating in a CUPID CARDS session should honor this vulnerability with patience and the faith that everyone comes to understand what we can when we can. Also, if people try to convince you that the answer to your question means something other than you think, trust your own inner wisdom first. It is the best counsel you have.

Finally, the question of fate and free will must be considered. Are the answers given by CUPID CARDS our final fate? What about our free will? If there is one thing that is certain, it is that our free will is stronger than anything. Hard work and awareness can change any situation. If you receive an answer that makes you unhappy or that you don't agree with, ask CUPID CARDS for advice on what you can do to alter your fate and triumph over the way things are.

One last note. Simply getting a favorable answer from CUPID CARDS will not bring true love into your life. The cards will help you only if you heed their advice and guidance and put them into daily practice. Remember, love, like life, is an art.

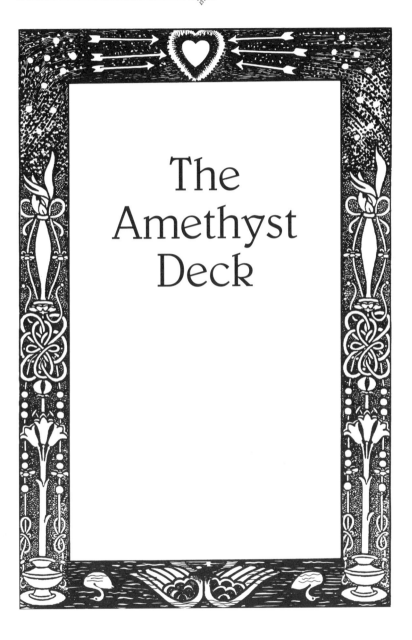

The Amethyst Deck

THE WARRIOR

A strong, vigorous man steps out of his protective foxhole, his wooden club poised to smite anyone who threatens the delicate heart he holds in his hand. He symbolizes the need to protect your heart from being broken or trifled with in any way. He has been pushed beyond the boundaries of his protective area.

 Circumstances require that the Warrior assert his right to live his life the way he wants. His aggressive stance may suffice for his purpose. However, he is prepared to do what must be done if appearances are not enough.

He is naked except for a strategically placed leaf, an undyed piece of cloth draped over his arm, and a battle helmet. The helmet protects his head and calls attention to the fact that this battle is primarily a mental one. His face is not covered; he is proud to let the world know he is ready to defend himself and stand up for what is his.

The leaf is a sign that his aggression is a natural phenomenon, like the lightning in the surrounding border. The lightning discharges tensions in the atmosphere. His bold, decisive actions will calm the charged atmosphere of a relationship that is suffering from an imbalance of rights and privileges, and from a lack of tolerance.

He has no need to be ashamed of asserting himself to protect his heart and home. The undyed piece of cloth also calls attention to his purity and lack of forethought. He has gone into battle cloaked only in the righteousness of his cause. He could have fashioned the cloth into a protective article of clothing, but he knew there was no time to waste.

Raised behind his helmet is the wooden club he has chosen over the swords and axe on either side of him. These metallic weapons are far too vicious and dangerous. Wood was once alive and holds stored energy. He is trying only to defend his right to be himself, not to harm anyone. Two empty helmets lie on the ground in mute testimony to the failure of those who would use harsh words and other weapons. They asserted themselves too strongly and destroyed each other.

The Heart of the Matter

The appearance of the Warrior in your reading indicates the question you asked is strongly related to how you express your own needs and how much of your time, energy, and other resources you allow a partner to demand of you. At this time, problems you are experiencing with your love life may be the result of your not asking either your partner, others, or even your higher self to give you what you are entitled to have. You may have a tendency to give too much of yourself and to ask too little of your partner in return. You may be more comfortable living both for the significant other person in your life and through him or her.

Too many people erroneously believe that love requires giving of yourself selflessly without expecting anything in return. One can only feel unsatisfied by this kind of relationship; it is not true love. In your heart, you know the loving relationship you seek is one where you and your partner give and receive from each other in equal measure. For this to happen, you must first identify what it is that you really want for yourself and then ask for it clearly and directly, knowing you deserve to get what you want and need.

When you practice standing up for yourself, you will finally see many aspects of your life come into harmony. You will be in a much better position either to improve your current relationship greatly or to find a new one that will bring you much peace and joy.

Problems you may now have regarding your love life may be caused by your fear that a loving relationship will require you to give up your own life with your own hopes, dreams, and desires. So you resist doing what you know you must do to bring this definition of a loving relationship into your life.

It may be true that your past experience of the word "love" caused you to feel smothered and imprisoned. But by changing your definition of what a loving relationship means into something you know you can live with, you will allow your higher self to bring such a relationship into your life.

THE JEWELER

A winged Egyptian figure takes tiny steps forward on a path leading from the sea with a treasure basket of precious jewels balanced perfectly upon its head. Even its wings are encrusted with jewels. While one hand steadies the basket, the other holds two linked rings of gold.

This is an angelic messenger come to inform you that you are on the right path and will have the opportunity to attain the kind of relationship you desire sooner, perhaps, than you thought you could. The strange form of this angel is to remind you that angels come in many forms, just as opportunities do. If you adhere rigidly to a preconceived notion of how things should go for you, you will probably not be able to see your opportunity when it arrives. It may not arrive the way you thought it would. Allow your higher self to use its infinite creativity to bring you the kind of relationship you desire in its own way and time.

Just as jewels are crystallized in the heat and fire deep within the ever-evolving earth, the relationship you seek requires patience over time. The two linked gold rings symbolize two wedding bands joined together forever. Like jewelry making, a successful relationship is the result of patient study, planning, skill, hard work, and a little luck. The appearance of the Jeweler means luck is running your way, so make the most of it.

In ancient Egypt, the scarab beetles in the border represented Khepera, the Sun god, who was so powerful he rolled the ball of the Sun across the sky the way beetles rolled balls of dirt across the ground. Symbolizing the goddess are the two sets of horns in the upper corners of the card. Each contains the disk of her symbol, the Moon. The bridge that arches between them symbolizes the twenty–nine and a half days it takes the Moon to go from full to dark and back again, a period we call a month, a word derived from the word "moon." The two symbols found beneath the bridge are among the most powerful in the Egyptian sacred tradition. Known as the Eye of Horus, they are a strong reminder to do good deeds, for the quality of your reward will depend on the energy you put out now.

The Heart of the Matter

The appearance of the Jeweler in your CUPID CARDS reading usually indicates that everything is going just as it should, even if it doesn't appear that way on the surface. Any problems you may be experiencing in your relationship are there for your own good. In the near or distant past, you were very helpful to another person with his or her love situation, and now you are about to reap the rewards of your good deeds. Your good luck may be manifesting in a way that seems to be making your life more hectic and confrontational on many fronts. Do not despair. These are areas in your life that need to be worked on.

If you find that your partner or someone you are interested in does not want to do the work necessary to make your relationship grow stronger, you should be thankful that you are finding out now while you still have time to do something about it. If there is no one in your life, the love you will soon experience will have been worth waiting for. By realizing present difficulties are for the best, you manifest the positive attitude that can bring a wonderful relationship to you.

The Jeweler means your greatest challenge now is to maintain a positive attitude when things do not appear to be going the way you want them to. As long as you continue to act and react properly, your positive outcome is virtually assured. However, if you find yourself in any dangerous or dishonest situations you must do everything in your power to get out of them. You do not want to waste the powerful good luck you have worked so hard to attain. The same energies that would keep you out of harm's way could bring you a fabulous love life if you let them.

Act as if good things are on the way. The ancient sages knew that our beliefs about reality mold and shape our experience of reality. And so your challenge is to remove all limiting beliefs and to concentrate on the fact that you are going to get the wonderful love relationship you have always dreamed of. It may come to you in a way you would never have imagined but it will come. In fact, it is on its way. All you have to do is follow your heart, taking small steps forward on your path, just like the Jeweler, and do what you know is right.

THE STORYTELLER

A seated woman pauses in telling the story of her life. She wishes to make certain that Cupid, seated at her feet, is still paying attention. To her delight, he is both interested and impressed, for her story has touched his heart. He gathers a basket of aromatic flowers, symbolic of his intention to bring her a loving relationship as

reward for her openness and the concern she has shown for his feelings.

She has been wise enough to play sweet music from her guitarlike instrument to set a pleasant and relaxing tone to her performance. She communicates a feeling of peace and tranquillity that is the result of the deep and empowering wisdom she has gained from her experiences. She knows full well that though there have been difficult times, they have made her strong and brought her to this idyllic place and to an audience with Cupid himself.

There is a sly look upon Cupid's face. He has given a secret command that has caused the clouds to rain down upon the Storyteller with the hearts of various lovers who would respond favorably to her tale. The birds in the sky have also been charmed by her story and have changed the course of their flight to bring her the best of these hearts.

The rainbow and the clouds that give birth to the rain of hearts are composed partially of dust suspended in the air, which allows water droplets to coagulate. Their humble origin does not diminish their ability to function in harmony with nature, or to delight us with their beauty. Though the reality of every story is never as perfect as poetic license allows it to become in the telling, each nevertheless contains a purity born of the necessity to make a good impression and provide the listener with an enjoyable experience.

The Storyteller knows her story is her personal myth and that, like all myths, its purpose is to help her make sense of her life. When shared with another, it can bring a closeness that may often lead to love.

The Heart of the Matter

In order to bring love into your life or improve an existing relationship, it is important that you enable others to better understand you by informing them of the people and events that have helped make you who you are. Your challenge is to tell your tale in a way that is interesting to you and your listener. This is not as easy as it can seem when a story is told by a skillful Storyteller. However, by turning your attention to the task, you will gain a perspective on your life and communication skills that you may now be lacking. This in itself can have a powerfully positive effect on your love life.

The art of storytelling is useless without the art of listening, and so you must remember to listen to your partner when he or she is speaking. Make sure you are really listening and not just appearing to do so as you think about what you are going to say next. Whether you are interacting with someone you have just met or talking to your mate of twenty years, there are few things as attractive about a person as the ability to listen well. Interest in what your partner has to say leads to sharing, and sharing leads to caring.

Conversely, there are few things as annoying as not being listened to or not being taken seriously. The appearance of the Storyteller is a reminder that if you and your partner are not interested in what you have to say to each other, you are not really interested in each other. You may be involved in a relationship based on practical considerations or physical attraction alone. This can lead to your feeling misunderstood and not appreciated for who you really are.

In storytelling, it is crucial to be aware of your audience. Therefore, as you examine your life in the presence of one who is important to you, ask questions about her or his life with a mind toward finding similar or related situations. When this activity is shared with another in mutual examination and personal exploration, it creates a close bond of understanding, which can lead to love.

THE NURTURER

Venus, the Roman goddess of love and the mother of Cupid, suckles him at her breast. Pregnant, too, she symbolizes the essence of the beauty of motherhood and maternal instinct. Cupid's father was not a mortal but Mercury, the god of communication. Having the gods of communication and love for parents, it is no wonder that Cupid is so skilled at bringing lovers together.

Above her right shoulder, Venus causes to appear a vision of the adventures Cupid and his fellow <u>amoretti</u> (Italian for little loves, the Renaissance term for the many emanations of Cupid) will have when he is old enough to sprout wings and fly away. By providing a sense of absolute security for her child, she enables him to look upon his future with confidence rather than apprehension. Infinitely wise, Venus knows exactly what her little one needs from her and offers it selflessly.

There are no manmade objects in this scene; even the little Cupids themselves are the product of the union of the immortal gods. Humans would not understand. In the seeming chaos of this utopian sanctuary is a perfection. Only Mother Nature has tended this garden, and her loving touch has brought forth beauty and growth in abundance. She knows each of her creations deserves life so it can fulfill its special purpose. Humans, on the other hand, would try to bring "order" to the garden with certain plants considered valuable afforded places of honor, while those plants whose uses are not known are classified as "weeds" and discarded. Mother Nature knows there are no weeds, only her children. Though we come into the world naked, Mother Nature loves us unconditionally and wants to give us everything we need and more.

This garden of Eden where Venus has chosen to suckle young Cupid is completely safe and secure. Not only the birds that hover overhead but the leaves on the trees join the flowers and animals in lending their support and protection to this microcosm. Similarly, by offering support and protection to another we emulate the divine force that animates the universe, the nurturing force of love.

The Heart of the Matter

You and your lover must demonstrate to each other that you are capable of giving and receiving unconditional love. There needs to be a sense that you can trust one another completely and can turn to each other for support and gentle guidance when one partner feels weak.

Look inside yourself and see if you are suppressing your maternal instinct when in the presence of one you care about. You may feel uncomfortable displaying this aspect of your personality, or you may not feel it exists in you. If this is so, there are many circumstances that could be causing you to feel so. Remember that a maternal nature exists in us all.

If your experience of the one who acted as a mother to you was unpleasant, or if no one nurtured, protected, and loved you unconditionally, you would not be clear about how to do so for another. Or you might think that "mothering" and "smothering" are the same. You might be reluctant to show your nurturing side to one who seems so independent, for fear you will be rejected.

Those who project an image of independence at all costs often desperately need support but are too proud or unaware of their neediness to ask. They act out their frustrations in the same way they did as children when they didn't get what they needed. The child we were still lives within us. Only now we are capable of causing a lot more trouble for those around us if they are not aware that we are in need of nurturing.

Like a mother with a stubborn child, sometimes you must just wade in and break through the wall of feigned independence and reach that child within who is calling out for help. If you find someone you care about who you feel is worthy of such a great expenditure of energy, make sure that he or she can pass this test: Either he or she has already done the same for you or you are quite certain he or she will do the same for you when you need it. Even the best of mothers has a hard time giving selflessly when her own needs have not been fulfilled.

THE LEADER

Two Native American leaders stand side by side discussing the best course of action to take for the benefit of the people who look to them for guidance. The strange, moonlit place in which they find themselves is symbolic of the darkness and confusion through which all leaders must navigate. The man stands proudly,

 looking off into the distance at a future that may or may not come to pass as he anticipates it. The woman is cautious and looks back, reminding him of the lessons they and those who have come before them have learned

The man wears a dual headdress, symbol of his rank. The feathers are from the eagle, the highest-flying bird, and remind him to look down from a higher perspective on all below. The horns, a symbol the world over for leadership and wisdom, connect him to the Earth, mother of all. On his tunic he wears the story of his accomplishments told in pictographs and the image of a circle divided into twelve sections, also a symbol found in the cosmologies of most of the Earth's people. It represents both the twelve signs of the zodiac and the twelve houses of an astrological chart. For thousands of years, leaders have guided their followers by the stars and planets. The orange circle surrounding this circle of the Earth is the symbol of the Sun, the great father who brings light and life to the earth.

The woman wears a necklace and earrings made from substances so precious they are also used as currency. Upon her chest are two beaded circles, the universal symbol of the Moon as she makes her transition from full moon to full moon. Thousands of years ago, the ability of a woman to create life caused all women to be seen as manifestations of the great goddess herself. For centuries women were held to be sacred, from the Latin sacer, meaning "untouchable."

These two Leaders are proud of their accomplishments, symbolized by their fine clothing, their tools, and, most of all, their partnership. They are wise but know how to listen. They are the archetype of all successful leaders. They harmonize their "male" logical left brain with their "female" intuitive right brain to make decisions that lead to the best results for all concerned.

The Heart of the Matter

The appearance of the Leader is an indication that your ability to assume a position of authority and control is crucial to your being able to bring true love into your life or make an existing relationship better. You are called upon to take control of your life—especially your love life—and lead, not just with words but by your example. If you think you cannot lead until you know exactly what to do, it is time you learned the truth the way every leader does—that is, by doing the best you can.

If you are in a relationship, you must be the smart one. Do what you think needs to be done. If you wait for your partner to take the lead, you will be disappointed. Your partner may have lost his or her way. Even if he or she appears resistant to taking your direction, in his or her heart of hearts he or she knows you are right and will come around to your way of thinking sooner than you think.

Your partner may need to feel secure in knowing you are

capable of providing strong leadership. Power is said to be the ultimate aphrodisiac. By displaying the power to take command, your attractiveness is enhanced.

If you are looking for a loving relationship, you would do well to cultivate an air of confidence and trustworthiness. Do not take shortcuts or get involved in underhanded activities. Behave nobly and with great style; it will benefit you in the long run.

It is especially important that you avoid appearing cheap or petty. Many people have a hard time accepting direction from someone who does not live up to a high set of standards. Therefore, present yourself as someone who knows the way, whether or not you are as sure as you appear to be. Completely trust that the combination of your logical mind and your intuition will guide you. It is time to be the one who volunteers to organize the situation for the benefit of all.

THE WORKER

All alone on her beautifully landscaped island, the Worker takes a moment to look her future squarely in the face. Her gaze is clear and direct but expressionless; she knows logically that she can expect little more than hard work to come for some time.

Her apparently serene demeanor is deceiving in more ways than one. On first glance, she appears to be standing still, leaning on her scythe for a much-needed rest. On closer examination, we see by the placement of her feet that she is actually moving forward. She cannot afford an idle moment; it is the time of harvest. She has invested much hard work in her crops, and to focus her attention on anything other than the work at hand would be ruinous. She is so obsessed with not wasting time that as she walks she is sharpening her blade for the harvesting to come.

Behind her stands a bird who is working hard at building a nest. In the border are two beehives and the indefatigable bees whose lives are dedicated to their own form of service. Crowning the scene is the Sun, whose tireless work brings forth grapes, berries, and all of nature's bounty. Though surrounded by the colors of nature, the Worker herself is drab and colorless. Her obsession with work has caused her to go beyond the purposeful business of the birds and bees and to move into the workaholic state that is peculiar to the "civilized" human race. She justifies her sacrifice by claiming to forgo the pleasures of life temporarily in order to produce them for a future time when she will cease her labors and enjoy their fruit. If her efforts are indeed part of a well-conceived plan for the future, she would do best to continue her singleminded approach and postpone gratification. Love and romance might distract her too much now.

However, if she is deluding herself about a future she is afraid to face, she may cause more harm to herself than good. She must confront the fact that she is not what she does. She must know she is worthy of love, laughter, and the enjoyment of the finer things simply for being alive like the birds and bees.

The Heart of the Matter

The appearance of the Worker in your reading is an indication that, at least for now, you should focus more on your work and career, even your hobbies, but not on your romantic relationships. This is a time when you would do well to ignore that aspect of your life in favor of financial and other considerations commonly referred to as practical.

If you are trying hard to improve an existing relationship, it is time to take a break from it. As the noted psychiatrist and guided imagery pioneer, Dr. Gerald Epstein says, it is time to "separate your intention from your attention." This advice holds true for accomplishing all goals. You may be surprised at the positive results you see in your relationship when you forget about it for a while. Perhaps you have been overly concerned about it or, just as importantly, your partner has perceived you to be so and is not happy about it. Focusing all that energy on other things for a while will allow you to be yourself. It will at least give you a new perspective when, and if, you return to "working" on your relationship. Your break from doing so may cause you to look at things completely differently.

If you are trying to bring a loving relationship into your life consider the logic of this advice. Assume there is someone out there for you. If you find yourself with people and relationships that do not satisfy, it is possible that, as of now, you are not the person the kind of person you are looking for is looking for. It is possible that by focusing on your career you will become that person. You may develop skills, resources, and attitudes resulting from your work experiences that will enable you to be more of who you really are. By completely forgetting about how you are perceived as a romantic prospect, you may very well project your most attractive qualities to the kind of person you have been seeking for so long. It is worth a try.

The important lesson of taking control of yourself in order to take control of your life applies to every one of the nearly two thousand different Cupid Card readings but even more so when the Worker appears. By not fearing to be alone you exhibit a very attractive strength.

THE LOVER

Two Lovers have stolen away from a social gathering and stand by the edge of a pond in the classic posture of lovers everywhere. Their mutual attraction is obvious but so is their tentativeness. Dare they hope this is more than a passing fancy?

They have devoted much time in preparation for this heated

moment. They have cleaned and groomed themselves with the finest potions and perfumes. The handsome man's beard is perfectly cut to signify that he is a gentleman and, presumably, not a threat to the honor and safety of this beautiful woman. He has reinforced this fact by being as charming and gentle as he is capable of being. To be otherwise would destroy the possibility of any affection developing between them.

Like the man, the woman is cloaked in a cape that blows in the wind along with her hair. The smell of the flowers in this sylvan glade mingles with the Lovers' perfumes to create a sensual experience they will both long remember whenever the wind carries the scent again. In a perfect moment like this we are reborn. There doesn't seem to be a reason in the world not to indulge our desire for pleasure.

Their clothes are likewise clean, of a flattering style, and made of the finest materials they can afford. They know that first impressions are very important, and so they want to highlight their best qualities and minimize what they think are their deficiencies.

These first hours of a romance are the most intoxicating of all. They are the stuff of epic poetry and plays. If love is the motivating force in the universe, than romance is the motivating force in life. This scene is that breathless instant when their everyday lives are transformed by the possibility that they have encountered their soul mate. At the very least, they are experiencing the heady pleasure a romantic encounter brings, a prime reason for living.

The Heart of the Matter

The appearance of the Lover in a reading is an indication that you should enjoy yourself to the best of your ability, making the most of where you find yourself. Though you may very well have met your soul mate, it would be best to put such thoughts out of your head and just concentrate on putting your best foot forward. Talk of marriage would kill the mood.

This is a time for being on your best behavior. Pay special attention to making yourself as attractive as possible in every way. Be charming and cultivate a sense of humor about everything, without being glib or silly. It is not a time for heavy discussions about the affairs of the world. Your affair is more important, and you should act that way.

If you have been seeking a loving relationship, prepare to encounter one in the near future. When Cupid's arrow finds its mark in your heart, you should enjoy believing the wonderful things you are hearing and feeling. Though you would do well not to take any foolish action you might later regret, grant yourself permission to take a break from logic and worry and to enter into the romantic world of the Lover for a time. It will be time well spent.

If it feels as though the romance in an existing relationship has gone sour, it is time to recapture what has been lost. A relationship incapable of recovering those indescribable feelings of excitement and exhilaration is in danger of failing. The Lover knows all too well that occasional romantic encounters are crucial in a lifelong commitment. The moment needs and deserves your full attention.

In either case, it is time to act as though life is a party to be enjoyed. Your lust for life will make you very attractive, and attractive is the key word when it comes to the Lover. You need not go out of your way to encounter the delights of romance. You would do best to make yourself, your possessions, and your surroundings as attractive and impressive as possible, and thereby you will draw to you what you have been searching for. To strive and strain in obvious effort to attain romance would work against you. Let the future wait and take care of itself. Worry and analysis would kill the delicate blossom of the budding of a romantic moment. It is time to be in the moment, experiencing romance with a gentle purity.

THE JUDGE

The heavy-lidded eyes of the Judge stare out and pierce through all veils of illusion and deception. Like the Greek god Pluto, the arbiter of whether souls went to the upper or the lower regions of the afterlife, nothing escapes his gaze or judgment. His long, flowing beard is a sign of his age and the wisdom time confers upon all who observe in quiet contemplation.

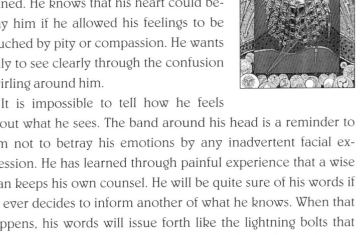

His concentration is so intense as to become hypnotic to all who gaze upon him. All they can see is his head; that is where the totality of his judgments is determined. He knows that his heart could betray him if he allowed his feelings to be touched by pity or compassion. He wants only to see clearly through the confusion swirling around him.

It is impossible to tell how he feels about what he sees. The band around his head is a reminder to him not to betray his emotions by any inadvertent facial expression. He has learned through painful experience that a wise man keeps his own counsel. He will be quite sure of his words if he ever decides to inform another of what he knows. When that happens, his words will issue forth like the lightning bolts that emanate from him. If those whom his words are directed to are not prepared to make use of his knowledge, then they will be hurt by it. Only those who are secure in their being can know that the Judge's pronouncements are not meant to harm and will profit from them.

If the Judge's words are not heeded, you can be sure he would never waste his time on that person again. He or she would cease to exist, for the Judge puts everything in its place, as symbolized by the circles surrounding the distinctive designs. Everything is itself or it is not. There are no in betweens. He does not do anything by halves or without passion. Despite the clarity of his decisionmaking, the Judge does not lack passion. There is a strong sexual energy surrounding him. While the upper two-thirds of his face show the nobility of his intentions, his lips reveal his sensuality. It is this that enables him to understand and identify with the most basic and even the basest concerns of humanity. His judgments are born of self-judgment and self- understanding.

The Heart of the Matter

The appearance of the Judge in a reading is an indication that you must be relentless in your pursuit of the truth. It is a confusing but important time, ripe for long-needed change.

This is not the time for pleasantries, tact, or beating around the bush. You are being called upon to look deeper into whatever situation you are in. It is crucially important that you face up to things the way they really are and not see them the way you would like them to be. Things may change for the better, but they will not change unless you ruthlessly judge yourself and your situation and act accordingly when the time is right and not before.

One possible scenario when the Judge appears is that someone may be lying to you or judging you falsely, and you must be careful to find out who, why, and how. Until you are absolutely sure of yourself, do not act differently from your normal routine and do not volunteer information, even to your closest friends. You may have to take some time to uncover the truth in order to combat the wrong that is being done to you. This way you can be absolutely sure of your situation before you act.

Another situation may be that you are involved in an obsessive relationship or one that has been transformed into a debilitating power struggle. If you have endured any kind of abusive behavior, the appearance of the Judge might mean you should begin to take actions calculated to help you make a clean break. You must face the situation head-on in order to protect yourself. You may even need to call in the power of the police and the judicial system to defend your interests.

On a more pleasurable note, the Judge can also refer to the art of seduction and sexuality in general. You may need to understand that cultivating an air of mystery would be a good way to attract the kind of relationship you are seeking. The qualities of the strong, silent type are indicated. If you must talk, whisper.

It might be a good idea to read a good detective story to refresh your memory about how a good detective has to think and act. There is a need for self-control in order to dominate the situation. If caution is not exercised, you may find yourself dominated by another. Judgment has its time and place. The place is where you are and that time is now.

THE ACTOR

A figure dressed as a geisha emerges demurely from one of the petals of an opening flower that is like the proscenium of a stage. She fans herself lightly, more for effect than to provide any cooling breeze. The fan in her hand is mirrored by those in the surrounding border, and they and the floating dragons heighten the theatrical quality of this scene.

In the plays of the traditional Kabuki theater, it is common for men to play the female roles. There is a strong possibility that under her flowing kimono, laboriously coiffed hair, and heavy makeup, this geisha is a man. It is good to look beyond our habitual system of classification based on our expectations and perceptions. For centuries theater has inspired and altered fashion, morals, and politics. Many ancient customs and traditions, good and bad, have withered and died as a result of being illuminated by their protrayal on the stage. Ideas that could not be stopped by force were often stopped by ridicule or general understanding.

What has motivated the Actor to take on the role of the geisha? Do the traits attributed to the geisha merit emulation and widespread dissemination? Or does the Actor feel the subservient, docile role associated with the geisha now needs to be held up to public scrutiny.

The geisha is the symbol of courtesans and people of both sexes whose life and livelihood depend on cultivating the attention and favor of powerful individuals. The role of the Actor is played by all of us at some time, but none play it more than individuals involved in politics. In China, you could tell a courtier's rank by the number of claws on the dragon that adorned his court clothes. Only the emperor could wear a dragon with five claws. The dragons on the card that hover around the Actor have three, the middle of the spectrum. The life of the courtesan was spent trying to stay balanced in the middle of the powerful forces swirling around the one whose favor was cultivated.

The Heart of the Matter

Often in life things are not what they appear to be, and this may well be one of those times. It is most likely appearances, not people, that are deceiving you. In any case you must question your assumptions. It will not be enough to trust that things are still the same just because you do not see how they have changed.

Appearances are important. Style is as important as substance, and you may have to pretend that you have much more confidence than you really have.

If you are looking for a loving relationship, you would do well to put on a grand show highlighting your strong points, your achievements, and your general desirability in every way possible. It may seem too demanding of your resources, but it will pay off in the long run. If you are uncomfortable with being recognized for your achievements or if you think you have none, this reveals a problem that should be faced and dealt with. Once again, the Actor can help.

If you are in a relationship, it is likely that your partner is unwilling or incapable of seeing and accepting the need for change in the situation that exists between you. In order to assist in this transitional time, you must not let on what you know to be true until it is clear that your partner can handle the stress involved. If it becomes obvious that your partner is never going to be able to handle the truth, you will have to leave.

Acting was one of the three holy arts of ancient India because the Actor imitated the divine spirit when a character was brought to life in order to depict a particular role in a drama. Furthermore, the ancient sages knew a powerful technique for achieving goals that has only recently been recognized and utilized again: The technique is acting as if the desired goal has been attained. The appearance of the Actor is an indication that you should act as if things are the way you would like them to be. This will alert and inform your subconscious mind as to how you would like things to be. The subconscious is powerful. You may see that things begin to move in the right direction as if by magic.

It is often said that the theater is a dictatorship, with the director acting as the dictator. It is no wonder that the Actor is legendary for knowing how to play politics. It is time for you to do so, too.

THE TEACHER

Wise in the ways of the world and beyond, the Teacher leans upon his staff the way his students lean upon his wisdom. He is tired of fools and has retreated to the peace and tranquillity of the forest. He has always learned much from patiently observing and contemplating the lessons, symbolic and literal, taught by Mother Nature.

Webs and nests are a lesson in architecture. Bird wings hold the secret of flight. Like the chameleon's colors, their plumage can attract or conceal. The ability of the snake, universal symbol for wisdom, to shed its skin teaches how we must all rid ourselves of things and ideas that have outlived their usefulness and thereby be reborn in each moment. The exquisite butterfly's transformation from the lowly caterpillar is a reminder that from our lowest depths we can still transform ourselves for the better if we become still for a while and listen to our inner voice.

The Teacher's eyes seem to look both far away and deep inside himself. He knows that his most precious wisdom comes from the universal intelligence that is inside and available to all of us. He did not learn this easily or quickly. He has traded the time he has spent since his youth in the pursuit of knowledge for a sense of peace that is beyond understanding.

He wears his age like a badge of honor; one does not survive long without learning life's lessons well. The amulets he wears are no mere adornments. They are objects of power. He has obtained many of them during peak experiences—times when life revealed its mysteries. Some contain herbal potions to heal or produce certain desired effects. Most precious are gifts from the woman who was his teacher for the Teacher is the living embodiment of the accumulated wisdom of many generations of teachers.

The Teacher possesses the many treasures that maturity brings. He is content in all circumstances. To those who seek to know the meaning of life, he possesses a beauty that surpasses all others. He will pass on all that he has to the few he deems prepared and worthy.

The Heart of the Matter

The appearance of the Teacher is an indication that it is important to act in a mature, learned, and wise way. For the best results base your actions on traditional methods and research. Pay attention to facts and figures.

In order to improve an existing relationship you should endeavor to improve yourself. Devoting time to self-improvement or study will enable you to change your situation for the better in many ways. If you find yourself in a relationship that is not satisfying intellectually, you must confront this fact and try to do something to put the relationship on track.

It is time to act in a parental role toward your partner but not a maternal one. You must be more interested in making sure your partner learns the important lessons you know must be learned than in seeing to it that his needs for nurturing are met. This is a time for serious conversations about practical concerns, not emotional outpourings.

If you are seeking a loving relationship you might want to consider looking for someone older or wiser than you. You might truly enjoy being in a position to learn from your partner. If that sounds unattractive to you, then consider playing the role of the Teacher to your next love interest. This might require being with someone younger than you, but not necessarily. In either case, your next relationship should have a definite element of the student/teacher dichotomy. Obviously, a relationship like this might start through a meeting in a library, museum, school, or other place of learning.

It is time to be with someone who is intellectually challenging to you. The desire to grow is one of our most basic needs. Literature is filled with tales of characters who have learned the hard way that you cannot improve your life in any meaningful way without growing in wisdom. You would do well to read more and learn about those who have worked to attain what you seek. Even your appearance should be that of a serious person who wants to learn more.

THE FRIEND

The prince and princess pictured in this scene are not brother and sister. Nor are they lovers, though they may become so in the future. They care deeply for each other and want only happiness for each other. But no romantic feelings have bubbled to the surface of the relationship. Perhaps there will never be any. For now, they are Friends.

It would be a mistake to call them "just" friends, because there is really no such thing. Their noble birth, symbolized by her crown of gold, his sword, and their exquisitely fashioned clothing, is a statement that friendship is the noblest relationship of all.

All crowns are a symbol of the rays of divinity said to emanate from great beings. This mental energy is seen by those of heightened sensitivity as an aura of light around the head, and its color, density, and intensity can be interpreted to reveal mental health and general state of mind. The sword carried by the prince is also a symbol for mental energy in the suit of swords in the cards of the tarot. Friendship, in this case, is ruled more by the head than by the heart.

The prince takes the princess's hand as he pledges his friendship at the bank of a great river. He seems to be about to take a step onto the river itself. Perhaps he thinks he has to walk on water to prove his devotion.

The union of their hands produces an electrical effect on their surroundings. A magic flower appears floating in the air between them, its petals opening and releasing a delicate fragrance. Their friendship, too, is unfolding, and its sweetness is beyond compare. The absence of the usual games played by new lovers has allowed them to truly know and appreciate each other. It is an energy that sends the clouds hurtling across the sky as if seized by delight.

Why has no love affair blossomed? Perhaps the merest hint of passion serves to strike fear into their hearts that their friendship will be destroyed, and so they repress it at all costs. They must realize that if their friendship is real, romance will only make it better.

The Heart of the Matter

Those who have accomplished much and acquired both great wisdom and great wealth will tell you that, besides their beloved families, their friends are their greatest wealth. The appearance of the Friend in a reading is an indication that how you feel about friendship will determine the quality of your relationship. Of course, most people enjoy the company of their friends, but the issue here is how you feel about friendship when it comes to a romantic relationship.

If you are involved in a relationship and friendship is not valued or present to any great degree, it is likely that the relationship will not last long. No matter how good the physical chemistry is or how exciting was the courtship, when the intoxication of the early days fades, trouble will start. The odds are that the infatuation was with the experience of a new romance and not a true joining of compatible people. Even if a relationship somehow endures without friendship, it is never completely satisfying, no matter what other needs it may serve.

If you are seeking to bring true love into your life, you should not dismiss the possibility that it may start out being a friendship. Whether it is with someone you already know or someone you have yet to meet, the relationship for you is one built on the solid foundation of mutual respect.

You may not be physically attracted to this person at first. You may display the all too common tendency to think that someone who is nice and kind is weak and boring. Too many people are looking for excitement because they think that is what love is. Real love is exciting because the two of you care so much about each other and show it in every way. To equate excitement with dangerous, inconsiderate, or obsessive behavior is to invite disaster into your life.

It will be best if you do not try to decide which of your old or new friends is going to be the one you are going to have a relationship with. Like friendship, your new relationship is going to grow at its own pace, based upon many factors, known and unknown. You will probably view your friends in a more appreciative light if you do not anticipate romance, and that more than anything will attract love to you.

THE HEALER

The Healer is an angel, a messenger from the divine. It is impossible to tell if this selfless soul is male or female. There is a radiance and a beauty about the Healer that transcends all notions of traditional sex roles. Only compassion and a desire to be of assistance animate this supernatural being.

The Healer does not merely offer but actually tosses us one of the many roses gathered in an upturned fold of this whitest of white flowing robes. This is to symbolize the active rather than the passive attitude all healers must have. The Healer knows prayer is important, but so are the actions taken in harmony with those prayers. Just as these protective robes are made of spun gossamer thread, the valuable aspects of our lives are woven by our actions to help another in genuine need.

The heart with six arrows approaching it that crowns this image is symbolic of the utmost love the Healer has to offer. Six is the number of healing. Each arrow represents Cupid's love taken to the sixth degree, going beyond romantic love to become the feeling the angels have for their mortal charges. Their sympathy is infinite; they know that, in the overwhelming complexity of human life, we usually forget our divine origin.

This complexity is symbolized in the intricate knots on either side of the Healer. They are not pulled tight but stand loosely, each supporting a vase. It is a reminder that a sturdy vessel made to contain the beauty of mortal existence rests upon a detached attitude toward life's complexity. By having faith that we do not have to tighten up to succeed in life, we turn away from our love of the world and back to our love of the great spirit that makes us all.

The Healer perceives the noblest and most deserving side in everybody, though lesser beings would see this as a lack of discrimination. Like the source of their divine messages, the angels work in mysterious ways. We must accept this.

The Heart of the Matter

The appearance of the Healer in a reading is an indication that how sensitive you are to your partner's needs and how you feel about putting your own needs second to his or hers will determine the quality of your relationship. The Healer goes beyond the parental role played by the Nurturer by requiring you to give your partner not what you think he or she needs, as a loving parent would, but what he or she really wants, within the bounds of your beliefs about right and wrong, even though you may not be in full agreement with them.

The Healer is the symbol of faith, but not a passive one. The Healer symbolizes faith in action—strongly held beliefs in the goodness of all that are then acted upon. There is always the risk that this kind of faith in another may turn out to be unfounded, but you are being asked to give it a try. Of course, if you feel you should not take the risk, you must follow your heart. In any event, you must heal yourself before you can help others heal.

Before any personal sacrifice is made to advance the interests of another, a thorough, honest examination of all motives involved must be made to see if such generosity is warranted. Focusing on the needs of others can be an escape from loneliness, the fulfillment of our own needs, or an urge deriving from the competitive side of life. Moreover, idealizing another can result from deception or lack of self-worth. The Healer is the most difficult persona to adopt. For this reason, it is especially important to make sure that the person you are willing to sacrifice for deserves it.

When you are in a relationship, the appearance of the Healer may mean that you must have pity on yourself or your partner. You must be the one to make peace. Lead the way in the exploration of healing practices designed to cure problems on the physical, mental, and spiritual levels.

If you seek a loving relationship, you may find it with someone less fortunate than you. You may meet in the performance of a charitable act. In any event, you must be aware of the tendency to idealize another for any reason. You cannot be the Healer forever.

The
Ruby Deck

INITIATES

A man stands resolutely, though fire appears to pour down around him from on high. He has waited long enough and has now decided to initiate his plan. He has no fear of the flames; fire is the ancient symbol of the energy available to us all when we decide to take action. His calm face belies the exhilaration he feels. He has

overcome the all too human tendency to do nothing but just wait and see. He has allied himself with the transcendentally powerful force that creates the entire universe in every moment. The excitement he feels is the emotional counterpart of the energy he has allowed to pass through him as he works his will on reality.

He holds his sword, symbol of the idea that motivates his plan, but he holds it pointed down. The time for ideas has

passed. Instead, he raises his left hand, and his desire to get things moving is so intense that a flame leaps out into the strange night sky. It is the first spark that will set the plan into motion.

The flowers in the foreground are the result of actions taken in the past. They stand before him with their beauty and beckon him to stop and smell them. However, he has decided that there is no time to waste waiting another moment. He stands upon ground decorated in sharply contrasting stripes, symbolic of the duality of his situation. He is either beginning his work or he is not. At this time of initiation, everything appears black or white, with no gray to confuse and delay.

Initiation is also the process through which someone is admitted to a club, rank of honor, or station in life. The initiation entails performing or, sometimes, enduring a predetermined ritual or series of meaningful actions. In this case, the man has had to go far outside the protective walls of his home. The flowerlike stars that seem to be falling from the sky that is their own home give this scene a transcendent feeling that seems to say what we are seeing is the most powerful of all initiations. Here is an individual who takes action in order to become more himself.

The Heart of the Matter

This card's appearance in a reading is an indication that taking action to get what you want is the key to bringing true love into your life and making an existing relationship better. You cannot make significant changes in your love life if you cannot overcome your natural resistance to doing what you know has to be done. If you can initiate action to improve your situation in spite of fears and insecurities, you will soon see positive results.

Fear of the unknown is the biggest obstacle to making a move. Even though things may be undesirable as they are, at least they are known. However, you must have confidence that you possess an innate ability to guide yourself on the proper course to achieving your desires. It is the power of your higher self. Your higher self communicates with you through hunches, flashes of inspiration, insights, and dreams. The language of dreams is symbolism, a most powerful force and one that operates in our waking consciousness as well.

The symbolism of this card is one individual taking a unique action without needing the approval of another. If you want to be first in your true love's eyes, you must be the first to make your move. In addition, you should act upon your first impulse and not second-guess yourself. Indecisiveness is incompatible with initiation.

You must consider what has gone before and, more important, what you are about to initiate, as a test of your commitment to having the best possible relationship. If you are to be initiated into the circle of those who have found their soul mates, you must not allow inertia, fear, or any other common obstacle to stop you from making the changes you know are essential.

There is urgency in this card. You cannot wait any longer, even though you may want to gather more information before you act. You must see your situation stripped bare of any elements that are not important and make your decision based only upon what is real and meaningful to you. If you would enjoy the passion of love, you must act first with passion.

MANIFESTS

A young woman stands with eyes calmly fixed upon us. She seems to be immersed in a stream of gently flowing water. The stream is symbolic of the ever-flowing images of our unconscious dream-mind, for though she is awake, she is using her ability to visualize the scene that surrounds her.

Her simple dress indicates that she may be poor or in a hospital. But her power of visualization is strong, symbolized by the aura that emanates from her head like a cap. She has seen herself in this, her favorite place, so many times and for so long that for all intents and purposes she is actually in this site of idyllic beauty.

She hears the songbirds and the water rushing by her to flow under the old stone bridge in town. She smells the flowers and the warm summer earth. She sees the swan who brings her a special flower to let her know that soon she will be standing where she has longed to be. Her patient, regular practice of putting herself where she would like to be has worked. Swans mate for life, and this royal bird is a sign that her soul mate will soon join her.

As if by magic, two delicately carved alabaster urns rise from beneath the flowing water. They are symbolic of the left and right halves of our brain. Their appearance on either side of this truly powerful woman is an indication that her brain's right half, the vessel of her intuitive, artistic side, and her left half, the vessel of her logical, mathematical side, are perfectly balanced. By harmonizing her brain's hemispheres she has harnessed the power of her being to create her own reality, not by her passing wishes and inspirations but by her deeply felt and visualized desires.

The peacocks in the lower corners of the card possess tails of almost unbelievable beauty, which they can suddenly spread to produce fear and awe in all who see them. Like the young woman, the swans, the town, and the two precious urns, they are tangible proof that reality contains numerous miracles that were once merely ideas in the mind of humans and of the divine.

The Heart of the Matter

Having this card appear in a reading is an indication that your ability to visualize how you would like things to be, your ability to make things become real, and the general tone of your moment-to-moment inner dialogue are the key to bringing true love into your life and making an existing relationship better. This is a card that speaks of your power to manifest the relationship you have always wanted—and more.

Since ancient times, those old enough or wise enough to learn the secret of manifestation have tried to teach it to those they cherished. It is a practice that is simple yet difficult. Simple because it requires you merely to decide what you want and then visualize it, not only seeing it with your inner sight but feeling it as if you were really there, experiencing it with all of your senses. Difficult because continuing to practice visualization every day at first, and then several times a day, requires discipline.

If guided mental imagery can help you manifest what you like, it should come as no surprise that daily visualization of what you do not like will, unfortunately, help you manifest that as well. This is why it is so important for you to become aware of the tone and subject matter of your moment-to-moment inner dialogue.

If you are focused on feeling angry at the wrongs done to you by your partner, others, or life in general, you will most probably manifest a continuation of those occurrences. If you continually think you are weak or unable to do what you want, you will reinforce that in yourself. Whenever you find yourself drifting back into old patterns of negative thinking, don't get mad; get even. Just smile at the tenacity of this nasty habit that is struggling to stay alive to hurt you, and know you have the power to defeat it. Then go back to visualizing what it is you want with all your heart. Do not wait until you are old to learn the truth of this. There's no time to waste.

COMMUNICATES

These two emanations of Cupid have just brought two unseen lovers together. They have taken a moment after their activities to sit on the bouquet of flowers picked by the lovers. They overcome their youthful shyness in order to talk about what they have seen and done. They want to do as good a job as possible, and by

comparing notes they can improve their performance. Here in this place of nature's delicate beauty, they can take the time to correctly analyze the subject without manmade distractions to interfere with their learning.

By their butterfly wings, we can tell they are in charge of bringing love to all things in natural surroundings, whether they be human, animal, insect, or plant. Like their comrades in the villages, towns, and cities, they know that not only love but gossip sometimes seems to make the world go around.

Their youth implies the innocence and the sincere desire to understand that should characterize gossip but often do not. The disembodied hand holding flowers above them symbolizes the gifts each has to offer and reinforces the fact that their communication is divinely sanctioned. Gossip can be the friendly exchange of ideas and information shared with the goal of enabling all concerned to grow in wisdom and live a better life. It is as natural to us as the desire to communicate love. After all, doesn't the contact between the butterflies and the flowers spread pollen far and wide, perpetuating future flower gardens?

The two Cupids look so alike they might be twins. This is symbolic of communication's ability to allow us to reflect upon and see our own way of thinking and being in the thoughts and words of another. Their body language offers us more proof of their inner state of mind. They lean toward each other like plants lean toward the sun, indicating their yearning to get closer to each other and grow in understanding. Their mutual interest in each other's ideas ensures that this will not be the last time they sit and talk.

The Heart of the Matter

When this card appears in a reading, it is an indication that your ability to communicate is the key to bringing true love into your life and making an existing relationship better. The difficulties we have with other people are usually the result of communication problems. Most often, problems arise because the parties involved are not making themselves clear to each other or because one or both refuse to listen. It is too easy to let fear and preconceived notions stand in the way of true communication.

Communication begins with an effort to make yourself clearly understood and to understand how your partner communicates. It is important to remember that the same words often mean different things to different people. This can be the result of cultural, regional, and age differences. It can also result from having our life experiences attach very specific meanings, both positive and negative, to words and situations we would ordinarily expect neutral reactions to.

For this reason it is important to look into the eyes of someone in whom you are interested order to get a general awareness of their inner feelings. Also, one can understand a lot about what is being said from body language. If your partner is looking or leaning away or folding his or her arms across his or her chest, he or she probably feels defensive or uncomfortable. Sighing or slouching can indicate a wistful or sad feeling.

When a reaction registers with you, it is often best to wait for an opening in the conversation and ask directly if what is being said is in fact producing discomfort. A caring attitude can bring immediate feedback as to how the other person feels about being open and intimate with you. This can lead to further exchanges or show you that you might have to look elsewhere.

If you are interested in a person, let it be known in a way both of you are comfortable with. It is amazing how interesting some-one becomes when we realize he or she is genuinely interested in us. Be aware that sometimes you may have to be obvious.

FORGIVES

A woman walks toward us with her eyes closed. In the lower left we see the thatched roof, foliage, and fence of the home she has just left. It is unclear whether she has just gone for a walk or has gone for good.

The appearance of Cupid flying frantically around her on the

back of a bird is an indication that there is need for two lovers to come together again soon. The other birds are also concerned; this is a relationship that they have seen work well, and they feel it is worth saving.

Her toga could be a common bedsheet grabbed in haste as she made her exit. The tray she holds has food for just one person. Perhaps she had brought two meals on the tray to her partner, but hurtful words passed between them, causing her to take her meal and eat it on her walk. Outside, in the steamy summer weather, she may find that a walk amidst the beauty of her neighborhood can remind her of the good times and good things in her relationship and enable her to cool down.

Cupid has thoughtfully brought a guitarlike instrument with him and plays the melody of one of her favorite songs. The words of the song are a reminder that the relationship that has just caused her pain is one she sought long and worked hard to sustain. Its haunting chorus causes her to keep her eyes closed as she walks, and she remembers other times when a careless word caused hurt and suffering. The rose that materializes at her shoulder is a sign that reconciliation is possible, though it cannot be bought merely with flowers but requires awareness that a genuine mistake has been made and that the lessons taught have been noted and slated for correction.

Through her introspective examination of her own behavior, she has decided that she has gone far enough and should return home. She has also learned from this and other experiences that in order for her to be able to forgive her partner, she must first be able to forgive herself. She must nourish herself not only with the meal that anger has delayed but, more important, with her divine capacity for compassion.

The Heart of the Matter

When Forgives appears in a reading it is an indication that your ability to forgive is the key to bringing true love into your life and making an existing relationship better. There must be forgiveness of yourself and others in order for healing and love to dwell within your heart. The energy you might channel into revenge will only work against you.

It is necessary to close your eyes to the irritating behavior of another if you are sure in head and heart that such an exercise of compassion will help another worthy of your forgiveness to grow. Mental, emotional, and spiritual growing pains are a fact of life.

The wise ones have known since ancient times that problems that manifest in our lives are frequently a result of problems we have been unable to resolve mentally, emotionally, and spiritually. If we are resistant to growing more fully into who we are, if we refuse to see the wisdom of changing our outmoded beliefs and attitudes, then we will manifest situations that force us to confront what was once an inner conflict. When that happens we either grow or retreat before the pain and suffering that inevitably accompany growth.

Forgiveness is the antidote to that poison which is blame. All too often, the tendency is not to try to solve the problem but to fix blame. Blaming someone provides a false sense of comfort to the one who is now absolved of any guilt or possibility of wrongdoing. If both people involved in a relationship are trying to grow, the odds are they are both capable of having made a mistake that now begs for forgiveness. It is not weakness but the greatest strength to forgive.

If you are trying to bring a loving relationship into your life, it is important that you forgive yourself before you go to sleep, especially for any past relationships that didn't work out. Accept your human frailty as a natural part of your being, and your mistakes as a sign of your efforts to grow. If you are not failing, you are not trying. The time of failure is the best time to plant the seeds of success. Make any potential partners aware of the fact that you know how to forgive.

CREATES

A woman sits lost in her sewing next to the raked-sand perfection of a Zen garden. Above her hovers Cupid, who is covering his eyes; he knows he has no business with her. Some time ago he brought this woman together with her true love. He has come to check on her because she is pregnant with a very special soul who is destined to do great things.

The girl doll beside this dexterous seamstress indicates that the child she is carrying is female. According to an ancient Japanese custom, the mother has begun to create the sash that this unborn child will wear on her wedding day. Like all creation, this lovingly made work of fabric art is a declaration of faith in the future. Like her child, this woman's work will take on a life of its own. The child will not only be wrapped in her treasured sash, she will be symbolically wrapped in her mother's love, faith, and skill.

The desire to give birth to something that has never been before is natural to both women and men. Since men cannot bear children, they must express their creative urges in other ways. The doll was fashioned by the child's father while her mother's body did the work of creating life. As supporting actors in the drama of raising children, men have traditionally done what they can to make life better for their family. Both parents have to be extremely creative to cope with the relentless demands of child rearing if they want to preserve their happy relationship. Even Cupid will be hard-pressed to devise a way to keep these soon-to-be parents together as caring lovers.

This has challenged human creativity since the dawn of

romantic love. Many lessons in parenting were learned by those wise enough to watch the animals and insects. The Greek myth of Ariadne, whose lengthy spun thread saved Theseus from the clutches of the dreaded Minotaur in the Cretan labyrinth, may be a tribute to the first wise woman who watched the nimble spiders weave their webs. We imitate divinity when we experiment and pretend and play with working our will. And as the spiders know, for a web begun, the Goddess sends thread.

The Heart of the Matter

This card is an indication that being playful, taking a chance, and exercising your creativity are all crucial to being able to bring true love into your life or make an existing relationship better. Whether you are already in a relationship or want to know how to bring true love into your life, you must play more.

Having fun is not wasted time. Make time in your busy life simply to play without looking for results from your fun, or you are depriving yourself of one of the main reasons for living. Cupid knows that not only is love a game; life itself is one, too. To demean the importance of games and fun is to demean the importance of life. The refreshing joy, exhilaration, and skills learned from play can help you solve your problems, especially problems with your love life.

Now is the time to explore your creative talents. The challenge is to recapture the sense of adventure, wonder, and playfulness that children possess. Children see a situation and ask questions and make statements that can enable an adult who thought he or she knew everything to learn something completely new.

Play this little game, and your reward will be true love. Look at your situation as if you were seeing it for the first time. Do not assume you know it all, but question everything with the bravery of a child, without fearing that you will bring up answers you may not like. What is really going on? How is it affecting you and your potential ideal love? If you could wave a magic wand and make anything happen, how would you want things to be? What is preventing things from being the way you'd like them to be? What, if anything, can be done to effect the changes necessary to eliminate what is standing in your way? You must start from where you are, examine your situation, and take a chance on yourself by making all changes that suggest themselves.

Creativity is equal parts intelligence, intuition, and heroism. Intelligence lets you examine and understand the problem. Intuition enables you to see a solution you might not arrive at logically. And heroism is required to implement your idea, along with more creativity.

WORRIES ABOUT

A woman walks somberly downhill with a faraway look in her eyes. She might as well be somewhere else; her worried mind is so preoccupied with the present difficulty that she is unaware of what is going on around her. The grandness of the cosmos, the magical shooting stars, and the music of the spheres have disappeared for her.

All her being is concentrated in her head, which gives off a powerful aura of colored light. The two flowers at her feet are symbolic of the solutions that are right in front of her. However, her attention is on what is wrong, and she looks as though she does not see them and will soon be tripped by them, possibly hurting herself.

She carries a box, a symbol of all the hurtful words that have been spoken in criticism of her and by her. She holds the lid down tight to keep them from emerging at this difficult time. However, it is almost impossible for her to carry this burden and deal with the present difficulty, for her self-confidence has been shaken and her worries make her too weak to turn around and go back to confront her situation.

In the distance stands her stone castle, seemingly perfect and impervious to any threat or outside force. However, the effects of perfectionism have breached the castle walls and wreaked havoc on the lives of the couple dwelling within them, as surely as an enemy army. She has been driven from the accustomed security of her home by the sudden appearance of criticism whose goal is destructive.

The opal moon that hovers strangely over the castle is a

reminder that stone can imprison beauty as well as protect it. It requires patience and delicacy to extract the opal from its stone matrix and fashion it into a precious jewel. Perhaps her partner will be moved by her disappearance to look skyward and see this message from on high. The lesson must be learned that peace begins where expectations end. You do not make anyone better by hurting them.

The Heart of the Matter

This card is an indication that how you deal with analysis, worry, and criticism is crucial to your being able to bring true love into your life or make an existing relationship better. Obsessive attitudes and behavior must be seen as a real threat to attaining true love.

Worry is the result of feeling that things are not the way they should be. Our attachment to expectations causes us to hold ourselves and others up to what we expect and to be critical as a way of getting things to be how we expect them to be.

Analyzing a situation is an important step to making things better. However, anxiety holds us rigidly in place, preventing relationships from growing, particularly when we yearn to know the perfect plan or the outcome of plans and actions before they have reached fruition. The unknown is always with us and must be embraced if we want to live a full life.

When we look back on what we used to worry about, it is easy to feel that most of our past anxiety was a waste of time. We usually deal more or less successfully with whatever circumstances arise. At its core, worry is a natural desire to protect oneself from pain by anticipating problems. However, you are also being practical and logical when you let your successes transform your life—and not your failures, real or imagined. Power can be gained by focusing on what has already been accomplished.

To expect and be able to live with imperfection, even failure, shows a realistic understanding of the material world. Criticism must be used for constructive purposes and not as a smoke-screen for hurtful words and deeds. Often, destructive criticism is a misguided attempt to deflect guilt onto another.

Conversely, reacting poorly to criticism prevents even the most constructive criticism from having anything other than a destructive effect. Negative emotions that seem to arise habitually in response to criticism can and must be analyzed to prevent misguided reactions to unfounded fears. Thinking and communication must be clarified and simplified to avoid misunderstanding and worry.

LOVES

Before you stands Cupid in all his glory. He seems quite proud of himself. His impish smile reveals his excitement with the gift he bears. He has ceased his restless flight and come to let you know that love will soon be yours. It is an honor not often dispensed by this capricious god.

In classical mythology, the other god-desses and gods are always represented as being of an age where affairs of the heart seem to be their preoccupation, yet Cupid is always portrayed as a child. Myths are made as teaching tools to help us make sense of our lives. The ancients knew that love is as precious, important, and fragile as a child, and so Cupid was singled out to be the only child among the gods and god-desses. Moreover, this winged cherub is a

subtle reminder that children should be the product of real love and not merely of base, carnal lust, a situation that plagues our age of "science" and "reason."

Symbols of new life abound here. Even the spring sky seems to be forming as it did on the first day ever. The newly emerged butterfly, just-opened flower, and unfurling ferns all sing of life renewing itself.

Cupid smiles so sweetly that on first glance you might not notice that his casually held torch is setting two hearts afire. Those two hearts belong to you and your love, and Cupid is fusing them. Love's passion, the fire that burns so hot it can sometimes consume unwary lovers, will soon ignite the kind of love you have been looking for.

The wings that fill the upper border of this scene are much

larger than Cupid's wings. Their gentle flapping fans the flame that joins your heart with another. They seem to be the wings of the many unseen angelic messengers who have helped Cupid guide you to your new awareness of love. This is an indication that what is coming up for you is quite special—the kind of relationship that can have a profound effect on the rest of your life. This mass of protective feathers will help you and your lover to take flight and soar beyond where you now find yourself and up to the place you know you are capable of reaching. It is time for love to bless your life.

The Heart of the Matter

This card is an indication that how you define and relate to love is crucial to your being able to bring true love into your life or make an existing relationship better. As love is the most powerful force in our lives, this card is the most powerful of all the CUPID CARDS. Its appearance in your reading means it is time for you to learn about real love.

What makes love different from, and more valuable than, romance or sexual attraction or friendship or service or any other of the aspects of life represented by the CUPID CARDS is that love contains them all and in their highest, most beautiful expression. You know you have found your soul mate when you enjoy just watching your partner live, when your desire to make your partnership work causes you, both to want to be there for each other in every way.

Romance is exhilarating because of its ability to bring out the best in you but, also because it is usually brief. Sexual attraction can be so urgent as to nearly overwhelm reason. It is not as pure an urge as the media would have you believe; it can be highly influenced by prevailing cultural trends and expectations. Friendship and service and healing and everything else are wonderful and have their important places in you.

However, when you love someone and he or she loves you, all these things and more combine in a way you cannot imagine until it happens to you. Your lover is your friend, and yet romance is only a glance away. Sexual attraction is heightened by mutual intimacy, trust, and commitment. When you love someone, you want to be with that person as much as possible, because at long last you have found him or her and life's brevity becomes starkly apparent.

Soul mates work on their relationship by working on themselves. When love is present, there is someone we can trust to advise us, someone who has our best interests at heart. In the company of a caring friend who will not leave us if we admit our weaknesses, we realize we are loved and admired and can examine the aspects of our personality that have given us pain. Love makes a sacred space in our lives where true growth and healing can happen.

TRANSFORMS

Two intricately carved stone pillars stand covered with strange, frightening faces and figures. Their maker is the stone carver, and we marvel at the result because this was a land without metal-cutting tools. Somehow, perhaps by strength of will or other magical powers, but certainly by skill and hard work, the stone carver

transformed raw stone into great art that embodied and conveyed great wisdom: the principle of human transformation.

To the unenlightened, these pillars seem to be of a time and place where human sacrifices were made to ensure fertility and success. However, as with all lost treasures, we must first clean the dirt of time and misunderstanding from ancient wisdom before we can use it. When we do, we see that these pillars are calling for us to give up our attachment to the habitual, self-defeating, and inappropriate aspects of our personality as we reach the heavens. They remind us that it is frightening to let go of the familiar and walk into the unknown of change.

The stone carver has chipped away at the raw stone for many moons, as symbolized in the upper border. In that time, valuable lessons have been learned as these sacred teachings were translated into art. The stone carver seems to have been transformed into stone to symbolize that we can "carve" ourselves into what we concentrate on. By doing so, we gain the protection of wisdom and success, as indicated by the winged helmet of pure gold, the most valuable of metals.

The chameleon mirrors the Moon in its ability to transform, a symbol of "as above, so below," the basic principle of alchemy.

Though commonly known as the misguided attempt by mad sorcerers to turn lead into gold, real alchemists try to transmute the lead of their base nature. The gold they work to attain is the precious wisdom resulting from the perfection of their own soul. An alchemist's heart is crystallized by the heat, light, and pressures of self-transformation. The flying heart on the card contains the multifaceted jewel called the Philosophers' Stone. Without it no alchemist can hope to change lead into gold.

The Heart of the Matter

This card is an indication that how you feel about change, especially your ability to change yourself and your situation, is crucial to your being able to bring true love into your life or make an existing relationship better. Change is the form of magic we are most familiar with, to the point where we forget that it is, in fact, a form of magic.

Magic is the art of working our will on our reality. Magicians study and practice techniques for transforming people, places, and things from how they find them into how they want them to be. By this definition it would seem that scientists, engineers, doctors, and psychologists are all magicians. Indeed, if we look back in history, we find that all these disciplines have their roots in arts and practices that were once considered the most powerful and feared magic. In fact, they are descended from a time when a culture's wisdom, technology, and religion were one and the same. Only the priests and priestesses were considered worthy of such powerful knowledge. It was potentially dangerous to the power of those in charge.

If you are in a relationship and decide you would like things to be different, you pose a threat to the status quo. However, a relationship that is incapable of changing is dying or dead. The surest sign of life in the natural world is growth and movement. By becoming aware of the need for change, you have started the process going. You must do your part, though the outcome is unsure. It is impossible to change others who do not desire change. You cannot wait for them. The present moment—the only time that exists—is your point of power. Work on yourself and, often, the results you achieve prod even the most rigid person to look at themselves with a view to improving their lot.

If you wish to bring true love into your life, this card is a call to prayer. Prayer is a form of magic in which we seek to ally ourselves with the divine. It puts us in an optimal mental and spiritual state, because we are acting with the goal of being in harmony with supremely powerful forces. Desiring this kind of right action makes all things possible. Do not let past defeats rob you of passion. The time of defeat is the most fertile time to plant the seeds of future successes.

SEEKS

These Cupids have realized that the time has come to leave the safety and security of familiar surroundings. Like caterpillars in their cocoons, they have been developing the strength and courage they need for the next stage in their lives. Now they know they must learn how to fly, and they have thrown themselves into it with unbridled joy and abandon.

Cocoons, nests, and families provide the supportive conditions that make growth possible. The younger Cupids help their older brother to take off first. He returns the kindness by taking them along until they are strong and skilled enough to fly on their own. The two youngest want to go but seem a bit reluctant to leave the safety of solid ground. At this early stage of flight, allowances must be made for those who are still learning.

However, once the lessons that can be taught by family and by accustomed surroundings have all been learned, it will be time for them all to go off on their own to seek their individual fortunes. If they do not, they condemn themselves to a life of limited experience and opportunity. Cupid's flight is more than amusement for him and is symbolic for us. Like all forms of travel, it offers a chance to see new places and witness strange customs, rituals, and ways of looking at the world that expand the definition of what it means to be alive on earth. Cupid teaches us that all creatures must continually expand their horizons to evolve.

The baby birds in the border of the card are using their fledgling flying skills to knit together ribbons and branches. This is symbolic of the way humans frequently learn new skills by traveling the earth and observing different customs and by watching how nature adapts in different places. The birds are even showing their departing Cupid friends what it means to tie a knot, something every budding Cupid should know. Life's search to experience the full potential of its being ties nature and humans together in complementary roles in evolution. This is how life comes to know itself. Seeking is a ribbonlike path that leads us farther and farther away from home until we get closer and closer to arriving at our true selves.

The Heart of the Matter

How you feel about learning, travel, and other methods for expanding your awareness of what is possible is crucial to your being able to bring true love into your life or make an existing relationship better. It is time to build on what has come before and find ways to make it better. You know you want things to get better, and they will. But to make the most of the energies operating in your life, you have to do your homework and seek out proven methods and techniques that are appropriate for the temperament of the CUPID CARD you picked previously from the Amethyst pile.

If you are in a relationship you want to improve, it is important that you take steps to expand your awareness of the world and its possibilities. Travel would be beneficial, but only the kind of travel that shows you new and different ways of being and thinking and allows you to be free of your mundane routine. Travel to see familiar people, places, and things would be detrimental. However, even a trip across the street can work wonders so long as it reveals new insights about living.

The technological marvels of our time make it a shameful waste not to take advantage of the almost limitless number of ways we can obtain useful information that helps us to grow. Travel, education, publishing, communication systems, and broadcasting can bring the world to us and take us and our ideas into the world. Attending the lectures and workshops of visiting experts, going to school, reading, and using interactive computer networks and various media sources are how you should begin your travels and be looking for ideas from experts and eccentrics.

If you are looking for a way to bring true love into your life, you must face the fact that you have a lot to learn about relationships, and take steps to do so. You may have to travel or otherwise go out of your ordinary circle to meet the one you seek or to find the right attitude for making your relationship work. It is time to use your wisdom to devise ways to learn more about yourself and your world. By doing so, you will become a more interesting, attractive person, one who is better able to recognize the traits necessary in one you want to spend your time with.

RESPECTS

A Chinese emperor is out for a walk in the parklike gardens that surround one of his many palaces. His opulent attire has taken many people much time to create and complete. Even his cane is made of rare wood from the Far West, a gift from a great explorer. The jewel embedded in the head of his cane is the largest of its

kind. And yet he has not paid for any of these trappings of fame and success. True, they are symbols of great wealth and power, but more impressive still is the fact that they and more have been given to him by his grateful people for the peace and prosperity he has brought to them. They are tokens of respect.

His word is law to the millions of people throughout his realm. He rules with fairness and wisdom. Streets and buildings and cities and whole provinces are named in his honor. Few know the meaning of respect as well as he does. He gets it from his subjects, from the lowliest beggar to the wealthiest prince of his realm, because he gives it back to them. His attitude of respect is such that he even steps around the flowers.

The magical cloud above the emperor shows that he knows respect is a gift from the divine, to be savored, learned from, and passed on, lest it swell his head with false pride. It is his nature to get and give respect because he respects nature, as symbolized by what he values and respects most: a very unusual bird whose song fills his heart with joy. He exalts this bird and holds it without grasping tightly, for he knows that to try to hold on to it would make it leave for good. He treats it as he himself would be treated by others.

The strange cloud sends out tentacles to caress this bird—the emperor would not let anyone call it "his" bird—and a magnificently colored butterfly. It is a reminder that the supreme shows us only the merest hint of its power in the great forces of nature upon which we depend and which the animals seem to understand so well. The emperor knows that his realm, his fame, and his life have limits but that love does not. He knows that love illuminates the darkness of a lonely world like the shooting stars in the border of this piece light up the night sky.

The Heart of the Matter

This card's appearance in a reading tells you to consider how deserving of respect you feel, and how willing you are to show respect for others, because both are crucial to your being able to bring true love into your life or make an existing relationship better. To make the most of the energies operating in your life, you have to ensure that you are respected for exemplifying the best qualities appropriate to the temperament of the CUPID CARD you previously picked from the Amethyst pile.

If you are in a relationship you want to improve, you must examine your existing attitudes toward authority and make changes if needed. Resentment of authority may prevent necessary actions from being taken. You may be reluctant to act as an authority because of negative associations with that role.

Sometimes we must defend the boundaries we have had to set in order to protect ourselves from invasive or other inappropriate behavior. If we do not feel we deserve to be respected and therefore have created good boundaries for ourselves, we are much more likely to suffer from the actions of others who need to be told they have gone too far.

If you would like to bring true love into your life, you must respect yourself and show that same respect for all you meet. If you find it difficult to respect yourself, be aware that the people you feel are most deserving of respect also have feelings of self-doubt. Doubt may never leave, but those who come to respect themselves learn to accept themselves as they are.

Beware of those who may display their unclear understanding of authority and respect through condescension or hostility. Remember to look beyond appearances to see such persons as they really are, for better or worse. If you do not, you should not be surprised if you are treated badly.

Many hurtful attitudes are the result of cultural egotism and prejudices blindly accepted as fact. Root out poisonous ideas in yourself, and be aware of them in others. Today's accepted attitudes and behaviors regarding the roles of men and women are quite distorted. Equal partners make successful relationships. There is no other way.

CHAMPIONS

A determined youth stands atop a hill with feet spread apart and a tunic billowing in the breeze. Even upon careful study, it is difficult to determine whether the youth is male, female, or experimenting with taking on some of the roles, values, and attitudes of the opposite sex. It is important for this youth to explore the limits of conventional mores and stereotypes; by doing so, personal tastes and the ability to stand up for unconventional beliefs and unpopular causes will be developed.

The youth seems to be looking down the hill and signaling to others below to follow in this escapade. They have not yet decided whether to join in the uphill march into the fiercely blowing wind. Not one but two arrows are held up in the youth's outstretched left hand, a symbol that people on opposite sides of the crowd are being called upon to fight against the prejudices inherent in their point of view and join together, so that truth may prevail, as symbolized by the single arrow soaring triumphant in the border above.

The youth holds the bow unnaturally tightly using the right hand. This is an indication that he or she is actually left-handed. Like many other left-handed and otherwise different people, he or she has always been made to feel uncomfortable.

This youth and many other people with special ideas and ways of being have had to confront culturally accepted standards and practices that were designed to enhance the personal freedom of the many but that for them serve only to inhibit freedom. Some meet the challenge of being different by accepting the conditions imposed by the majority. Some become overwhelmed by their situation and give up. Unafraid of being different—to the point of being proud of it—this youth has had enough of the status quo, symbolized by the cracked columns of a ruined temple, and has chosen to rebel and demand equal treatment and opportunities. The vision of how things ought to be is a call to arms that cannot be ignored.

The Heart of the Matter

This card is an indication that how willing you are to be the champion of unpopular, unconventional, and downright eccentric ideas and people is important to your being able to bring true love into your life or make an existing relationship better. To make the most of the energies operating in your life, you have to ensure that you are willing to come up with a new and different way to express the qualities appropriate to the temperament of the CUPID CARD you previously picked from the Amethyst pile.

Now is a time for exposing yourself and others to unusual viewpoints and theories, and maybe even unusual experiences, too. Think, say, and do what you want without fear of embarrassment, contradiction, or rocking the boat. Avoid censoring yourself or others, and be especially careful of those who would like to censor you. You simply must stir things up a bit.

Prepare for a time of extremes, and expect the unexpected. Be aware that what seems like an accident, mistake, or failure may be an opportunity for achieving the love you want by an unusual route.

A false sense of security built on denial of what is really going on is unacceptable. Though this is a time of rebellion against limitation in all forms, it is best if your actions are preceded by a dispassionate, scientific examination of the way things really are in your life. Be aware that sorrow and anger may arise when the negative effects of the status quo are fully realized. Remember that fighting the established order will be more difficult if you must also contend with your own anger. Care must be taken to not eliminate what is good when eliminating the bad.

It is not easy to rebel against conventional wisdom and bring much-needed change to your love life. However, it is rewarding to do so. In addition, to resist taking action against a situation you find intolerable only delays the time when, inevitably, you will act. Do not let fear of ridicule or the fear of reversing old beliefs and ways of behaving stop you. It is time to discover the latest ideas and unconventional methods for bringing more love into your life.

ENDURES

A woman looks out from a crescent moon. She seems to be staring sadly at a beautiful angel hovering among the plants and flowers of her divine realm. The angel, however, is bowing her head, seeming to want to avoid direct eye contact with her mortal charge. She knows why this poor woman's face has appeared to

her as if in a tortured dream. The woman has been praying for the strength to endure the difficult time she has been having. She has looked deeply into her soul, symbolized by the crescent.

The angel's bowed head and hands are held up in a gesture of warding off the woman's pain. It hurts to watch this human who is so dear to her suffer. However, she knows there is nothing even an angel can do to change the fact that, in many ways, life is a veil of tears, symbolized by the veil that spins out of the angel's right hand to envelop the woman and the Moon. Those who have been born into this world are as distant and isolated from each other as the Moon is from the Earth.

The force of gravity keeps the Moon spinning around the Earth, providing mysterious illumination and beauty and serving vital functions like regulating the tides and the cycles of plants, animals, and human beings. In a way, gravity is a symbol of love, which also pulls us closer to one another and strives to keep our lives together.

Both angel and mortal must remember to stop and smell the flowers that are growing in great profusion. There will always be challenges that threaten our equilibrium, and so to balance our pain and discomfort we must remember to be aware of the beauty around us and inside us. Endurance, when practiced consciously as the character-building lesson it is, gives us time for valuable and much-needed self-reflection. Our life moves only at the rate at which we can deal with it. To deny this truth is to invite things to change in an even more unpleasant way.

The Heart of the Matter

It is important for you to be realistic and patient during the sustained effort needed to bring your desire for love into reality. To make the most of the energies operating in your life, you have to endure the natural obstacles that will arise even if you are able to exemplify only the best qualities appropriate to the temperament of the Cupid Card signifier you previously picked from the Amethyst pile. Whether or not your reading has been graced by the appearance of the Jeweler, you must be able to wait the short time it takes for love to enter your life. Heed the lessons of this card well; when you are waiting, time seems to pass very slowly.

We suffer mentally when we want things to be as they are not. However, there is goodness in things as they are. If you appreciate that, you will find it easier to endure what you are going through. By understanding and accepting the greater purpose behind your present circumstances, you will also be able to be more alert to opportunities you might otherwise have missed.

Enduring is a spiritual practice to be used only when the goal you want to reach and the circumstances you must experience are in keeping with your values. You do not have to endure unfair or poor treatment. There is no benefit to enduring a violent or abusive situation.

Though your goal is true love, you must realize that you cannot attain it without also cultivating the quality of patience in yourself and with others. The ultimate goal is not pleasure or excitement but contentment in all circumstances. We can know true contentment when we embrace the present and stop struggling to escape insecurity, pain, and doubt.

When you finally attain that which you seek, you will find a whole new set of things you must patiently await. Decide now that you will develop the ability to endure, even in the face of not having everything you want. If you do not, success may appear to you to be always in the future, or in another's power, and you will never really enjoy your life.

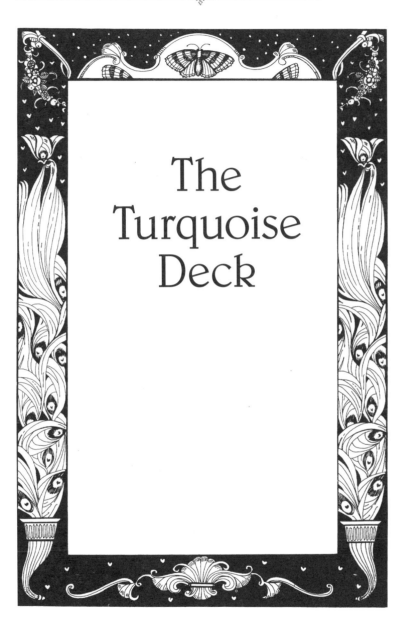

The
Turquoise
Deck

SELF-ESTEEM

A woman walks down a garden path clutching a mass of flowers in an upturned fold of her toga. She has flowers under her arm and a floral wreath in her hair. Like the flowers she holds, she glories in her beauty in a most natural way. She has developed self-esteem, a most valuable possession, by listening to her

higher self, as symbolized by the shining eye seen in the hand-mirror to which she directs her gaze.

She has used self-reflection to understand her strengths, symbolized by the man, woman, and Cupid in the other three hand-mirrors, and her weaknesses, as symbolized by the fences she walks before. She has decided to listen to the bluebird who says happiness will come when she grants herself the same respect she would to any other who displayed similar characteristics. The bluebird knows life can be enjoyed by using our strengths to compensate for our weaknesses.

The pointed rocks behind her symbolize our tendency to be too hard on ourselves. She has gotten beyond these stumbling blocks, and the flowers she holds, as well as the ones that cover the top of a stone column in the border above her, are signs of the great rewards that will come to her as a result of new actions born of her newfound self-esteem. A self-confident person is like a magnet whose force field draws other positive people.

At her feet, a tiny Cupid grabs the hem of her dress and reminds her not to keep her head so high that she cannot see the path in front of her. Self-esteem, not egotism, will get her where she is going.

Behind her floats a winged face of Cupid. The faceless wings in the border above have been summoned by Cupid and are flying toward this woman and the lover that this cherub of love has chosen for her. Cupid's eyes are lifted toward heaven, the ultimate ground of being. We can all feel good about ourselves; we are all of divine origin. If we are not proud of ourselves, we are not proud of the divine force that made us, the world we live in, and love itself.

The Heart of the Matter

This card's appearance means that Cupid wishes you to emulate the qualities indicated by the card you selected from the Amethyst pile, and to do so in the manner indicated by the card you selected from the Ruby pile, while keeping in mind that your ability to maintain this course of action is going to depend on your attitude toward self-esteem. Without self-esteem, you will not feel worthy of the love you seek and will sabotage even the best efforts of yourself and Cupid.

Your level of self-esteem is based on how much you respect yourself. All too many of us have been conditioned from early childhood not to think highly of ourselves. Parents, siblings, and others often say and do things that lower our feeling of self-worth. As we mature, we fear being thought to have a "swelled head." This leads to being afraid to feel good about ourselves, which in turn, leads to a whole host of problems that manifest all too clearly in relationships.

In an existing relationship, problems with self-esteem can manifest in two ways. A person who exhibits low self-esteem can be manipulated by a partner willing to take advantage of his or her tendency to be all too willing to think the other knows better than he or she does. On the other hand, sometimes a person with low self-esteem becomes a belligerent know-it-all to hide the fact that he or she feels worthless inside.

If you manifest or encounter either of these attitudes, then you must realize that a loving relationship is not possible until change occurs. The people you bring into your life are a reflection of how you feel about yourself. If you are confident and respect yourself, you will not tolerate anyone who treats you poorly. If you have grave doubts about yourself, you will not respect anyone who tells you of your good qualities. You will attract those who focus on your weak points, because you will think them smart enough to see through your facade, brave enough to confront you, and caring enough to tell you about your foibles. Often people who are happy to criticize or point out your faults to you use this tactic consciously or unconsciously to manipulate others. By convincing you of your unworthiness, they are only masking their own feelings of inferiority. A loving relationship requires both partners to have self-esteem, so that they may then exhibit esteem for each other.

DESIRE

A man and woman stand frozen with desire for each other. Each is a cultural stereotype of the way far too many people feel about what they need in a romantic partner.

The woman is pretty and blond, dressed in a diaphanous gown more suited to seduction than anything else. She is the archetype of the woman who uses her sexual attractiveness as her primary method of making her way in the world. In her right hand she holds two large flowers as a symbol of her rank and station in life as an object of beauty. Her stance is a coquettish mixture of beckoning her partner to come to her and fleeing from him at the same time.

The man is dressed in the splendid garb of authority. His phallic crown and the apron he wears seem to call attention to his position as exalted above other men. He, too, is an archetype. He is the man who uses his power and wealth to attract the attention of one he desires. He reaches out his hand, not to touch her but to show her she is permitted to touch him. He would not be able to have a relationship with a person who did not acknowledge his position of leadership and control.

It is a fair question to ask if either of these people would have anything to do with each other were it not for the wealth and status they hope to derive from possessing and being possessed by each other. The king cobras at the base of this scene turn away in disgust.

Some people justify this kind of avaricious quest for dominance, power, and prestige by comparing it to the mating practices found in some members of the animal kingdom.

However, to do so is to ignore the fact that true love gives the gift of divinity to human beings.

The gold coins being blasted out of the machines on either side of these two is a reminder that values can be manufactured. The plants below these machines are papyrus, from which the Egyptians made a form of paper that has, in our time, tried to combine the value and usefulness of gold to form paper money. However, just as the value of paper money is an idea placed in our minds by politicians and currency traders, the values these two confused individuals are displaying may be the result of their having succumbed to cultural conditioning from earliest childhood.

The Heart of the Matter

This card is an indication that Cupid wishes you to emulate qualities indicated by the card you selected from the Amethyst pile, and to do so in the manner indicated by the card you selected from the Ruby pile, while keeping in mind that your ability to maintain this course of action is going to depend on your attitude toward desire. The desires that have caused you to ask your question of the CUPID CARDS are the first ones that should receive your scrutiny.

If you are in a committed relationship and have asked how to improve it so that it measures up to your desires, this card can mean you must make sure you are not asking for more than you can reasonably expect at this time. Or you may be asking for things to change in such a way that you would find yourself dealing with consequences you have not taken the time to anticipate. In addition, you may not have realized the things you will have to give up to effect the changes you desire.

If you are trying to bring a loving relationship into your life, the appearance of this card in your reading has additional meaning. You may be looking for a person with certain qualities that, upon closer examination, are desirable largely because of your cultural conditioning. The reverse of this problem might also be true. The people you are attracting to yourself may be responding to signs and behaviors that have more to do with who you think you should be than with who you really are. Naturally, in the latter case, people would not be relating to you as you really are, and this would cause you to strain your resources to keep the charade going or unconsciously create ways to free yourself.

In any event, you cannot get what you want if you do not know what it is that you want. The appearance of this card in your reading is an indication that you must be very clear with others as to exactly what it is you want from them and what they can expect from you. If you cannot, you will only end up acting on your lusts, those base desires which, without reflection, can drive your actions and can result in grave consequences.

DUALITY

Two men, who are so similar in appearance that they must be twins, are locked together in a wrestling match. This does not appear to be for sport but seems to be a serious attempt by each to force the other into submission.

Throughout mythology, fights between brothers have been  portrayed as particularly fierce. However, in this scene neither brother has the upper hand. Each is applying strength in equal measure to the other and, consequently, there appears to be no movement; they appear frozen.

Only one can be the victor, as symbolized by the one great bird that flies around the two combatants at close range, but which one will it be? The smaller birds in the border are anxious about the result because they have taken sides in this matter, as revealed by those in the left border being lit and those in the right border being masked in shadow. The outcome of this contest, too, is masked in shadow.

In the top border are two stylized eyes, symbolic of the fact that though one eye can see, two eyes will permit depth-perception. Symbolically, the two eyes tell us to seek a more in-depth view of a situation by trying two different and unique vantage points from which to observe what is going on. Depth is also simulated in this scene by the lively background that seems to recede into the distance. A feeling of depth can be attained by letting our eye wander over the scene depicted and observing the different objects—the large flower at the lower edge, the wrestlers above it, the bird above them—from several points of view.

In the bottom border, two fists seem ready to pound a soft

heart between them. This is a symbol that the human heart can take only so much argument before actual physical damage occurs. However, the strain caused by the anxiety of not knowing how the situation will progress can be even more detrimental to our health than the strain of fighting.

The Heart of the Matter

This card's appearance is an indication that Cupid wishes you to emulate the qualities indicated by the card you selected from the Amethyst pile, and to do so in the manner indicated by the card you selected from the Ruby pile, while keeping in mind that your ability to maintain this course of action is going to depend on your attitude toward duality and decision making.

Since ancient times, great thinkers have concluded that duality is the central organizing principle of our reality. We cannot know what light is unless we know darkness. We cannot know the meaning of sweet without knowing the meaning of sour. It follows that we cannot know what we like without also experiencing that which we do not like. For this and many other reasons, the material world will never be a place where one quality will prevail over another.

Poor decision making is the common denominator of all human problems. Consider how we all make decisions. We try to accumulate as much information as we can, but we never have as much as we would like to have. As the deadline to make the decision approaches, we hold our breath and make our best guess. We become more proficient at guessing from training and our experiences, learning about the experiences of people we respect and admire, and through the use of techniques that develop our intuition.

If we are not aware that the ever-changing nature of the universe is reflected in our lives, we are certain to be disappointed. In order to find and keep love in our life, we must embrace duality, especially in the form of the often startling differences we find between us and another. Accepting these differences as valid points of view enables us to learn from others and enhance our own life.

An option often ignored yet available to us at all times is remaining undecided. Many times the problems indecision would cause are far less serious than those caused by a premature decision. It takes great courage to admit that, for the time being, it is best to decide not to decide.

THE PAST

Under a darkening night sky, a Cupid has come to a beautiful but lonely place. Hovering before him is a winged head that looks like one of his kind but is not. This is the form taken by the angelic messengers who bring news from on high to the Cupids of the world. This higher being has come to inform Cupid of the consequences of his past experiences.

The clouds grow even darker as Cupid learns that he was not born with many of the personality traits he has come to accept as his. His early childhood experiences with his mother, Venus, the goddess of love, and his father, Mercury, the winged-footed god of communication, have had both good and bad influences on him.

His days of blithely bringing lovers together without thought to the consequences of his actions have resulted in many unions that have been successful and a few that have ended in pain and regret. It is not easy for such a free spirit as Cupid to admit failure, but it is time for him to learn and grow and move on to greater challenges.

As he learns from his past, he gains perspective on his life as a whole. He starts to look less like an infant and more like a young man/god. Though his wings grow smaller, he rises to new levels of enlightenment. His new self-awareness is symbolized by his self-conscious attempt to cover his nakedness, like Adam and Eve. Even Cupid matures when he confronts his past.

We are witnessing a momentous occasion. This Cupid has been going about his business of love for what seems like many centuries, and he is ready for the new chapter opening up in his life. He can no longer act without relating his actions to what he has learned from the past. He has learned that, though his childhood is now over, it still lives on in his memories and in his very being. As he continues to walk through the garden of life, he will be more aware of his patterns, and, for the most part, he will avoid getting stuck by the thorns of plants that have hurt him in the past. Confronting the past is a right of passage that every thinking being must endure.

The Heart of the Matter

This card is an indication that Cupid wishes you to emulate the qualities indicated by the card you selected from the Amethyst pile, and to do so in the manner indicated by the card you selected from the Ruby pile, while keeping in mind that your ability to maintain this course of action is going to depend on your attitude toward the past.

If you are already in a relationship and trying to make it better, the past can have a great influence on whether or not you will be able to do so. Many of the things that are preventing your relationship from being as loving as it can be are the result of attitudes, habits, and actions that have their origin as responses to past events in your life and in that of your partner.

If you are trying to bring true love into your life, you must ask a trusted friend to help you identify habits and attitudes that do not seem to go with the rest of you. The nature of habits is that we are usually unaware of them, and so a little loving outside help is needed. This is also a way for those in a committed relationship to help themselves if their partner is unwilling or unable to help them. Those with a commitment problem are usually afraid of experiencing a repeat of an unpleasant definition of commitment they encountered in the past.

What used to be an appropriate way of dealing with stressful situations may be quite inappropriate now that you are older and know better. However, it is the nature of habits to rule us unless we first become aware that they are habits, examine the events that gave rise to them, and become aware of how they actively influence us. The only way to eliminate a habit is through patient awareness and the belief that your life will change for the better if you stop acting in the old habitual way. The chances of making your relationship the best that it can be are greatly heightened, if you and your partner remain ever wary of how habits born in the past may be affecting the relationship, and if you come to see the value of this essential part of growing in wisdom and maturity.

ROMANCE

On a hill overlooking a town square, under the watchful gaze of their guardian angel, a woman and a man stare into each other's eyes with obvious romantic longing. They are dressed in clothes of a most romantic design, the kind we think of when we think of princes and princesses, for these two, like the red rose that opens

slowly at their feet, are symbolic of lovers throughout history.

Their guardian angel hovers over the rooftops of the town blowing a trumpet, hoping to alert these two lovers and wake them up to the fact that this wonderful romantic fling has the potential to turn into something even more wonderful, the reunion of two soul mates. For this reason, they must not abandon themselves totally to the quite natural bliss derived from the meeting of two people whose chemistry is right. The hearts that litter the ground in the border below them are mute testimony to the loves they have each had and abandoned in the past and to the loves the world over that have faded. This romance may be just another one of them. On the other hand, it may be that a true love has been found at last.

The appearance of the many planets with their moons, as well as the Moon herself, in the border surrounding these lovers is symbolic of the very unusual, dreamy quality that comes over us when we find ourselves involved in a romance. Even a place lived in for years looks strangely different when seen through the eyes of one in love.

At first glance, we see only planets and no stars in the night sky pictured in the border of this card. However, on closer examination, we find that a few dark stars can be seen in silhouette. This odd juxtaposition is actually closer to representing the real positions of the stars and planets in relation to the Earth, for the stars are actually millions of times further from us than are the planets. Yet it appears to the naked eye that the opposite is true. Romance, too, enables us to see, with unusual clarity, the truth about life. It produces a new appreciation for its fragile beauty that does not diminish but only grows when romance turns into a committed partnership.

The Heart of the Matter

This card is an indication that Cupid wishes you to emulate the qualities indicated by the card you selected from the Amethyst pile, and to do so in the manner indicated by the card you selected from the Ruby pile, while keeping in mind that your ability to maintain this course of action is going to depend on your attitude toward romance.

The appearance of the Romance card in your reading shows that conditions around you are right for you to bring a new level of passion to an existing relationship or to become involved in a new romance for those who desire one. Furthermore, please keep in mind that though there is never a guarantee that a romance will blossom into a committed relationship of the kind you desire, the chance for this to happen is greatly increased by the appearance of the Romance card, especially if either the Lover (Amethyst deck) or the Loves card (Ruby deck) also appears in this spread. If all three are present, true love is surely at hand.

Romance is surely one of the most intoxicating of feelings possible which is both its wonderful attraction and a cause for a bit of caution. There is a tendency to throw caution to the wind and to overlook warning signs about a person you are romantically involved with in the belief that love will work things out for you. It is important to remember not to go against your better judgment. You can only change yourself; you cannot change anyone else. You can, however, make sure you are getting involved with a person who is desirous of changing themselves for the better. Also, Having a sense of humor is a tremendous asset when it comes to being romantically involved. It is one of the most valuable and attractive features a person can have. It is also a trait that can be cultivated through honest observation, but many people are not willing to be honest about themselves. If you can keep looking for the humor in your situation, not only will you find it, but it can get you through practically any difficult time.

Through the centuries, romantic myths and fairy tales have tried to show us what the ancient sages knew to be true without doubt: that men are willing to go through a lot to earn the appreciation of their true love and that women, as the keepers of the sacred flame of life, desire to be given the respect they deserve. If it feels easy and natural for you and your partner to demonstrate your mutual appreciation and respect, there is a very good chance that romance will blossom into a deep, true love that will last a very long time. You will have found your soul mate.

SERVICE

Appearing as frozen in place as a statue, a man stands poised in the eternal position of sowing the seeds for a future bountiful harvest. At the bottom of this scene are symbolic images of the ordered rows of crops that will soon spring from the seeds sown by this tattered but honest tiller of the soil. His clothes are made from the cotton, wool, and leather that he himself has grown, shorn, and tanned. The buildings behind him were fashioned from trees he cut down and milled himself. His seeds are the result of his skill and foresight, gathered in the past to ensure his survival. Even the basket from which he disperses his seeds is a vessel he has made himself.

In the not too distant past, when the majority of people spent their time working the land to survive, a scene like this was as common as eating. Today it is almost never seen. Yet, a farmer sowing seeds is a symbol so basic and essential to our daily life, on physical, mental, and spiritual levels, that statues of this noble farmer should be erected in places of gathering throughout the world, instead of— or, at least together with—those of warriors, something all too many farmers have been forced to become. In any event, it is both farmers and soldiers who give their all so that others may be safe and sound.

Surrounding his head is the flaming halo of the Sun's aura. This farmer is up with the dawn so that the many people who are still asleep in the village behind him will eventually reap the fruit of his labors. Just as the sun gives life to all, it is the efforts of those willing to put their short-term comfort second to their long-term goals, that enable many others to survive.

In the uppermost border is another halo, only this one represents the spirituality emanating from this scene of pure harmony with the rhythms and cycles of nature. The farmer does his best to assist fruit trees, flowers, and crops to propagate and flourish. It is no wonder that the Sun crowns this simple farmer with life-giving golden rays. The jewel-encrusted symbols of rank sitting atop the heads of world rulers pale in comparison to the crown that ennobles this farmer and his service to humanity.

The Heart of the Matter

This card is an indication that Cupid wishes you to emulate the qualities indicated by the card you selected from the Amethyst pile, and to do so in the manner indicated by the card you selected from the Ruby pile, while keeping in mind that your ability to maintain this course of action is going to depend on your attitude toward service.

There often comes a time when one partner must put his or her own needs second to the other's, though it may seem like this goes against what you know to be true about the equality necessary in a truly loving relationship. Of course, if this imbalance goes on too long, or if the partner providing this service is asked to do things he or she is not willing to do, the Service card can indicate that the relationship can begin to appear as frozen as the farmer whose form illustrates its meaning. The reappearance of the Sun, in the form of a counterbalance of loving service provided by one's partner, can thaw out the situation every time, if true love is really there.

Like farming, service is hard work. For this reason, the appearance of this card means that love will enter your life through your job or career. Also related to farming are food, exercise, health, and hygiene. Attend to your personal hygiene, clean up the details in your life, and make sure that anyone you are interested in does so as well. Those matters are even more important than they usually are at this time. Improve your cooking skills. Learn the inseparable relationship between what you eat and how you feel. Work on fitness and you will be more attractive and in a position to meet other fit and attractive people.

Service to another must be given freely and with love, or it is not service but servitude. When love is present, you enjoy knowing that you are helping your partner to live to the full. It is equally rewarding to use your strengths to compensate for any weaknesses your partner has. When these energies are flowing back and forth freely, you will come to know a level of pleasure in life you have never known before. The Service card actually holds the secret of true joy and happiness in a committed relationship.

PARTNERSHIP

A man and a woman stand on the shore of their own private lake. Their regal bearing and fine clothes mark them unmistakably as members of the high nobility. This is further confirmed by the castle tower behind them and to the left. It is from its raised gate that they have come to stroll through their magnificent grounds.

They are blessed, even more so because they know they are, and they are humbly thankful to the divine forces that animate them and their world.

The woman has her full attention on her partner. She has her hand on his shoulder, offering comfort and support. The man loves and trust her totally; he would not turn his back on anyone else in his realm. He knows that she is always there for him, standing behind him in whatever he does. He has infinite respect for her wisdom and guidance and freely admits he could not accomplish anywhere near as much without her. She is his greatest strength.

Her sense of self is such that she would not allow anyone else to turn their back on her, but she knows he does so only because he seeks to find a lovely flower for her hair and, in every other way, to delight her. She feels the depth and power of his love and respect. Like her, he is totally devoted to making their world a satisfying, safe, and secure place where they can be themselves fully. This makes her love and respect him even more. Together, they have served as living examples that have inspired many.

The special rainbow that now shines so magnificently down upon their realm was not always so strong and bright. It is a symbol of the work they have done, on themselves and on their world, to grow like their beloved trees, flowers, plants, and vegetables.

The single ray that illuminates them is a symbol of the one love they have shared and wish to share forever. It is nothing less than true enlightenment, which they have gained by seeing the divinity in each other, even when times were difficult. The butterfly lit by this ray represents the transformation they have gone through together. They have exchanged youth and enthusiasm for the rarest treasures: trust, true peace, and the timeless quality of love existing between soul mates.

The Heart of the Matter

This card is an indication that Cupid wishes you to emulate the qualities indicated by the card you selected from the Amethyst pile, and to do so in the manner indicated by the card you selected from the Ruby pile, while keeping in mind that your ability to maintain this course of action is going to depend on your attitude toward partnership. The opportunity to become closely involved with another person who may very well be the right one for you to share your life with is now in the cards for you. This card can also mean that a celebration of commitment is near, whether it be a traditional marriage, an engagement or some other arrangement of the partners' own choosing.

A romance is a celebration in and of itself, but a partnership justifies the celebration of a whole circle of friends and families, because it is truly the greatest experience possible to us as human beings. When you are in a real and loving partnership, the teachings of the world's great philosophers come alive in a way that cannot be explained to those not fortunate enough to have experienced true partnership. Words like cherish, caring, patience, trust, and sharing take on new meaning.

If you are in an existing relationship, this card is a call to hold it up to the high standards of a real partnership. Of course, no relationship ever attains perfection and stays at that level. Envisioning an ideal gives us a goal to work toward. Working toward goals together is the essence of a living, breathing partnership. However, if achieving mutual trust, honesty, respect, and equality seems impossible, you may have to confront the fact that the good partnership this card might be indicating is not the one you are presently in but the next.

If you are seeking to bring love into your life, you must be careful not to let your knowledge of what a partnership is interfere with the natural progression of any budding romances. Do not expect your romance to exhibit the qualities of partnership too soon, but do pay attention to whether the romance has some of what it takes to grow into a real partnership. The bonfire of romance is replaced by the hearth fire of partnership only through patience and hard work.

SEX

A beautiful, angelic youth stands before us in the first blush of sexual maturity. It is Cupid himself, or at least it was Cupid. We see him here in a form never seen before. He looks up wistfully at the tiny cherub that has now taken over both his name and his former job of bringing lovers together. Now it is this little one who shoots his arrows into the hearts of lovers, while our young angel is preoccupied by other thoughts.

The candles on either side of this scene represent the two sexes. The purity of the sexual act is symbolized by their brightly burning, heart-shaped flames. Calling attention to the necessity of keeping love in the sexual act are the heart-shaped smoke rings that float upward to try to circle their cherubic master. However, the little one sits in a large fan, which he uses to prevent the smoke of desire from enveloping him.

The sexually mature form of Cupid embraces his desires, because he is mature enough to transform them into a beautiful union with his true love. The butterfly, universal symbol of transformation, breaks through the largest of the smoke rings, calling attention to the fact that sex is a most natural thing.

The act of sexual union is obviously part of any divine plan to keep all the species of our lush, fertile earth evolving. However, this universal symbol of life has suffered greatly at the hands of those who are afraid of its power, because it in some way threatens their own puny sense of power. The force of the urges of sex is so strong as to tear away the mask, seen behind the candle on the right, of anyone who tries to deny it in themselves and in others.

When combined with true love, sex is one of the highest forms of expression. It is then a great creative act, symbolized by the child's face at the base of each candle. Without love, sex becomes just another way we avoid feeling empty. Sex without love only keeps us in pain and unaware of our divinity.

The Heart of the Matter

This card is an indication that Cupid wishes you to emulate the qualities indicated by the card you selected from the Amethyst pile, and to do so in the manner indicated by the card you selected from the Ruby pile, while keeping in mind that your ability to maintain this course of action is going to depend on your attitude toward sex. In this day and age, great care is needed to make sure you are ruling your sex drive and not being ruled by it.

Centuries of strongly enforced though completely unnatural prohibitions against sexuality repressed our most basic human sexual urges and led to a general attitude of sexual rebelliousness that has obviously gone too far for anyone's good. The unnaturalness of sexual prudishness has been echoed by equally unnatural and ludicrous sexual perversions in a seesaw battle between victims of both of these untenable and, ultimately, boring persuasions.

Lost in the quiet of the happily balanced middle of this devastating conflict are those who know, but do not speak of, the joy they derive from experiencing sexual union with their beloved.

Only this experience can generate a force as powerful as the lust both prudish and lewd people flock to, like moths to a flame.

Morals are currently not fashionable, for fashion is driven by economics, and economics is driven by things other than morality. We have a situation where the sexual urges and identity of most people have been shaped to a great extent by the forces of sexual repression and the consequences of that repression. Unfortunately, because of this, it is important for every person in our "civilized" society to closely examine all aspects of his or her sexuality. We must all do the work of rooting out in ourselves the corrupting influences of a culture that is only now emerging from the dark ages of repression and ignorance.

We are being challenged by the real circumstances we find ourselves in to refrain from having sexual relations until we are certain in both head and heart that there is a true and potentially lasting bond possible. The reward for this is real sex, real power, and real intimacy.

TRUTH

Beneath a dark, forbidding mountain, the unusual sight of a woman with the wings of a butterfly greets our eyes. She walks a path that seems to be lit by a supernatural light emanating from her. Her glowing upper body seems to be pushing back the darkness surrounding her. She symbolizes Truth, which also has the

power to push back the darkness of lies and ignorance, to show everything to us as it really is.

She is a special angel whose domain is the earth. Her gaze is direct, serene, and not clouded by self-doubt, though she lacks the compassion of some other divine beings. Her butterfly wings tell us that truth is a natural thing to our universe of opposites. Truth has evolved out of it like a simple caterpillar evolves into the butterfly crowning this scene.

Unlike the pure divinity of the world beyond the physical, truth can come into being only in this place of light and dark, good and evil, truth and lies. In this divine place there is only a kind of truth that is beyond words and human understanding, as startlingly beautiful as the peacock wings on either side of her. The peacock feathers floating out of the border represent the expansion of our minds when we search for the truth. In our search, we travel far and wide in our imaginations to come back to that core of our own being which holds our truest essence. Peacocks are proud of their beauty, just as Truth is proud of the paradise she lives in. The colors here are vivid and clear, for clarity holds the key to obtaining truth.

She holds a wooden box in front of her heart, the place used in the symbolic art of most cultures to symbolize both love and the telling of the truth. Inside the wooden box is the gift of Truth. After love, Truth is the greatest gift that one person can give another. Without Truth, there can be no real love.

In this box is a deck of CUPID CARDS, which also have neither a top nor a bottom. They are symbols of the truth, because they put you in touch with your higher self, which knows the truth about you and your life. She holds it in a special way. She is putting her energy into the cards so that we will understand and know the truth when we hear it and see it.

The Heart of the Matter

This card is an indication that Cupid wishes you to emulate the qualities indicated by the card you selected from the Amethyst pile, and to do so in the manner indicated by the card you selected from the Ruby pile, while keeping in mind that your ability to maintain this course of action is going to depend on your attitude toward telling the truth and knowing when others are telling you the truth.

It is said that there are no heroes and heroines today to act as role models, but that is incorrect. It is a heroic act whenever one partner gives the other the gift of truth. There are many couples that practice such heroism, and you probably know one. They are people who know beyond doubt that they have found their soul mates. They are some of the most fortunate people on earth. When you have taken the time and done the work of establishing mutual truthfulness and trust, you will find that it frees up an incredible amount of energy that can be used to accomplish many important things.

You cannot be truthful with another person unless you are first truthful with yourself. It is important to examine your motives for signs of self-deception before you do the equally important job of examining the motives of another. This is work that must be done, both in an existing relationship that you want to improve and in a meeting with someone who interests you.

Cultivating the habit of telling the truth to yourself enables you to be truly present in your relationships. Once again, freeing up the energy required to deceive yourself and others enables you to really enjoy yourself, which other people always find attractive.

It is very important to be open to hearing the truth, whether or not it hurts to hear it. Though it may be unpleasant, the truth can set one free from the consequences of living a lie. Rather than dismiss what makes you feel uncomfortable, it is best to open up your mind to the possibility that what you are being told may be true, even if only from the point of view of the one who is speaking. Being open to this possibility is a sign of your respect for truth. In time, respecting the truth will become a habit in your life and in your relationship.

REPUTATION

Two marvelously attired women stand side by side looking at a scene taking place outside the frame of this image. They are lost in an animated conversation about this event and ignore the approach of the wondrous planet Saturn, symbol of time, patience, discipline, and of their rewards. Saturn also represents the law of karma, which states that for every action there is an equal reaction. It is a law that applies to planets, rocketships, and people.

These are no idle gossips. The butterfly wings on their backs are an indication that they are angels and speak only the truth. They are guardian angels, and their job is to observe their precious chosen ones so they may see what they can do to help. Some of the things they see make their job easier, but many things make their eyes grow wide with wonder. Things that seem important to their earthly charges seem most curious and of dubious value to them. They are the very spirit of compassion, as their cheerful demeanor attests, and they observe without judgment.

The guardian angels have, for their own amusement, adopted the garb of courtiers in a palace of the ancient Middle East. The purple leaves in the sky around them are the symbols of good actions they would like us to do to create a purple aura of protection around us. In the sultan's harem, the reputation of his wives and concubines was supremely important, even a matter of life and death. Gossip among the courtiers was not only a way of life but a medium of exchange.

Here on Earth, those who observe us usually judge us with a

harshness born of their own displeasure with aspects of their personality. The sketchy border of this scene is like the sketchy ideas and fantasies that gossips trade with each other about who we are, what we are doing, and why. When they are malicious in intent, nothing we can do will change their ways. However, that does not remove our responsibility to do our best to ensure that our reputation is an asset, not a liability.

The pagodas in the border are symbolic of palace life, the crucible in which the fire of the ruler's actions mixed with the politics of the advisers, nobles, and courtesans. The seat of any government or company is often a place where one's reputation can sometimes be more important than one's actual accomplishments.

The Heart of the Matter

This card is an indication that Cupid wishes you to emulate the qualities indicated by the card you selected from the Amethyst pile, and to do so in the manner indicated by the card you selected from the Ruby pile, while keeping in mind that your ability to maintain this course of action is going to depend on your attitude toward telling the truth and to knowing when others are telling the truth to you. It is also very important for you to establish a reputation for being someone others can rely on.

You must do everything you can to make sure that what is said about you by those who matter to you is favorable to your reputation and that of your partner or someone you would like to be your partner. The best way to insure your reputation is to make sure your actions are in keeping with your highest ideals. You cannot do more than that.

This card may also mean that you should conduct a thorough investigation of your partner's reputation. If you discover allegations of misconduct, remember that they may be false. Be sure that your sources have a reputation for reliability.

You must act as if you are being watched by your guardian angels. You must avoid doing anything you would not want them to see. This card can mean that the partner you seek is looking for someone with a good reputation, someone who is reliable and knows how to play the game of politics. Reputation can also refer to status, social graces, manner of dress, and financial resources. All these things are going to be a major factor in making your relationship the best it can be.

This card may indicate that you must examine how much reputation figures in how attracted you are to an individual. You may be attracted to someone for what they do, instead of, who they are. This can obviously lead to long-term problems. If you are having trouble with a person because of either of your reputations, try to make very clear what is true and what is false. You can count on the fact that what you have done, good and bad, is going to come back to you.

The Future

A guardian angel soars out of a cloud and pulls back a corner of the curtain draped along the top of this scene. Standing behind the curtain is an equally celestial being dressed in fine robes tied around the waist with a belt woven of solid gold.

 The robed and helmeted figure is the Future. The angel has dared to pull back the curtain that hides the Future from the present, because the mortal he cares for is in despair and has prayed fervently for guidance about what path to take. The angel has gone so far as to point out the direction he would like to see the future take for his poor, long-suffering charge.

The Future takes no notice of this angel, who has exposed what should be secret. The Future walks its own path in its own direction and in its own time will reveal itself. His golden belt symbolizes that the future of all creation is woven from the individual strands of our own private future. The angel is forced to confront the fact that even with such powerful wings and divine powers, the future can never be fully revealed. The future of an individual is part of a divine plan, and the individual directs his future as part of that plan.

The Future holds the treasure of life and other gifts within the large box in his arms. The Future is a box that can be opened only with patience, practice, and the right key.

The angel knows that if his human charge develops on all the levels of mind, body, and spirit, the proper destiny will come into reality. Each moment contains the potential for more probable futures than there are puffs on the surface of the clouds in this scene.

Some futures are more probable than others, as symbolized by their different shapes and shades of color. By gaining a thorough understanding of a situation and examining it with relaxed contemplation, flashes of intuitive insights can result. They illuminate the proper course to be taken in the future, if our mind is truly open to whatever may come. Even so, the Future is always being created, so we must always retain respect for the Future's ability to manifest in unexpected ways.

The Heart of the Matter

This card is an indication that Cupid wishes you to emulate the qualities indicated by the card you selected from the Amethyst pile, and to do so in the manner indicated by the card you selected from the Ruby pile, while keeping in mind that your ability to maintain this course of action is going to depend on your attitude toward the future and the unexpected turns taken by your relationship and other events.

We will all be affected in unforeseen ways by unforeseen events. Unless we can accept this fact of life and have confidence, we will experience anxiety. Having faith in ourselves and in the power of our higher self to bring the right experiences into our life at the proper time can help us to cope with this anxiety, which arises from time to time even in self-confident people who have devoted a lifetime to developing their faith in themselves and a higher power. The power of the future is the power of the unknown at its most basic and awe-inspiring.

Some people do not give much thought to the future, especially the future of a romantic involvement. They think that planning eliminates spontaneity and takes the fun out of things. They do not want to be bothered imagining even the most basic consequences of their actions. An extreme of this is engaging in unprotected sex. Those who engage in less self-destructive but still risky behavior think the future will take care of itself. They are right. However, when the future is left to take care of itself, it often does so in an unsettling and sometimes unpleasant manner.

Problems occur for several reasons. First and foremost is the lack of preparation for events that could have been foreseen. In many cases, this can be enough to prevent major life disruptions. However, it is obvious that even the most thorough and precise execution of the most perfectly thought-out plan must leave room for the unexpected to occur, because it always does. One of the few things about the future that can always be counted on to occur is the unexpected.

ISOLATION

A kind, gentle, and sensitive woman steps ashore and inhales the sweet aroma of the first flower she has held in a long time. In its fragrance comes a momentary escape from her recent sea voyage and all the cares of the world—and she has known many. In fact, she has known such sorrow that she has chosen never again to see, hear, or otherwise encounter anything or anyone that can cause or even remind her of her pain. In her all-consuming passion to stay away from anything but what she considers to be ideal, she has run away.

Offshore lies her great ship, symbol of her willingness to journey to the ends of the earth to avoid what has become intolerable to her. The ship has not anchored but drifts around in a circle. If she does not like what she finds here in this new place, she can always return to her vessel and sail away in her neverending search for a place that is as wonderful as she can imagine. However, she must be careful that her isolation lasts only as long as it should.

Perhaps this time her journey has led her to her personal paradise. Here, the sun does not burn the skin, and the moonlight does not confuse the eye. Instead, both luminaries have been replaced by a strangely hollow orb that seems to be emitting a most unusual kind of light from blue-black flames jumping off its circumference. Its circumference, in turn, is stranger still: It appears to be made from the rings of the planets Saturn or Uranus. In this place of refuge, the stars are not distant but seem close enough to touch, as they add their own light to the scene.

The only things that seem familiar are the creatures of all shapes and sizes that surround her, from the one-celled animals and strange sea creatures at her feet to the sea birds above. The single star that floats in front of the clouds as they roll in is a symbol that this world is the dreamlike vision of a single person. Also, just as the polestar is used by sailors to navigate, so are our dreams, fantasies, and idealizations essential to us when they are used as lofty goals that, nevertheless, can help us to arrive at the best place we are capable of reaching.

The Heart of the Matter

This card is an indication that it is important for you to put distance, either emotional or physical, between bringing true love into your life or making an existing relationship better. To make the most of the energies operating in your life now, you have to keep your distance, in order to protect yourself. It is crucial that you avoid being overwhelmed as you begin to express the qualities appropriate to the temperament of the CUPID CARD signifier you previously picked from the Amethyst pile.

If you do not put distance between you and those around you, you may find it hard to distinguish between your feelings and theirs. Choose only to be around positive people. Those who are intoxicated, sad, hurt, or angry have the power to hurt you if they do not calm themselves or if you do not remove yourself from their influence. In any event, you must protect yourself from the insensitivity of others. Isolate yourself from your routine to get in touch with your true feelings. This can mean travel, if only for a few days. You may need the release of a good cry, which can act as an escape valve for your emotions.

Isolation comes in many forms, and it is up to you to chose the appropriate method. If you are trying to make an existing relationship better, you may find it beneficial to work on becoming emotionally detached, or you may find it necessary to leave the relationship, temporarily or permanently. Sometimes making a strategic withdrawal can give you time to rest and recover your perspective. You may be surprised at how different you see things when you are not stuck in the middle of them.

If you are trying to bring love into your life, it may be a good idea to go somewhere where you can be completely cut off from your daily routine. You must be careful to stay out of your own way. If you do not put distance between yourself and your lack of satisfaction with your love life, you may unknowingly sabotage yourself by responding habitually instead of being genuinely present. Becoming a lonely victim is a form of escape, but it will not get you to where you would like to be.

PICTORIAL INDEX

The CUPID CARDS are presented alphabetically below.

The Actor
page 40

Champions
page 83

Communicates
page 59

Creates
page 65

Desire
page 93

Duality
page 96

Endures
page 86

Forgives
page 62

The Friend
page 46

The Future
page 120

The Healer
page 49

Initiates
page 53

Isolation
page 123

The Jeweler
page 19

The Judge
page 37

The Leader
page 28

The Lover
page 34

Loves
page 71

Manifests
page 56

The Nurturer
page 25

Partnership
page 108

The Past
page 99

Reputation
page 117

Respects
page 80

Romance
page 102

Seeks
page 77

Self-Esteem
page 90

Service
page 105

Sex
page 111

The Storyteller
page 22

The Teacher
page 43

Transforms
page 74

Truth
page 114

The Warrior
page 16

The Worker
page 31

Worries About
page 68

Pictorial Index • 127

BIOGRAPHICAL NOTE

When artist Amy Zerner met writer Monte Farber over twenty years ago, an enchanted relationship was formed. Since that time the two have married and become the world's foremost designers of interactive divination systems. Within the last eight years, Amy and Monte have created six divination systems or self-transformation tools, three children's books, a coffee-table art book, an album of music, and a CD-ROM series, which they refer to collectively as "spiritual power tools." There are over one million copies of their books in print in nine languages.

Amy Zerner is the first and only artist working primarily in fabric collage to win a major National Endowment for the Arts fellowship grant in the category of painting. Amy's unique talent as an imagemaker results in art that is based on inner visions, dreams, myths, and fairy tales. Her work combines textiles, embroideries, papers, and assorted found objects to create visionary images intended to act as signposts to spiritual growth and healing.

Monte Farber distills the results of years of studying mythology, philosophy, astrology and other ancient wisdom into a form easily understood by today's audience. In addition to being a writer, Monte is an inventor, musician, agent, promoter, and, of course, interpreter of Amy's images.

Through their work together, Amy and Monte have helped people around the globe to make their inner world a more beautiful and empowering place, so that they are better equipped to deal with the frenzied pace of modern life.

To comment on your experience with CUPID CARDS, write to:

Zerner/Farber Editions, Ltd.
P.O. Box 2299
East Hampton, N.Y. 11937

For information about other projects and forthcoming events, including exhibitions of the art of Amy Zerner, please include two first-class stamps along with your name and address.

Also available in bookstores from Penguin Studio:

Karma Cards: A New Age Guide to Your Future Through Astrology
by Monte Farber   ISBN 014-015487-6 Price $12.95